AF378758

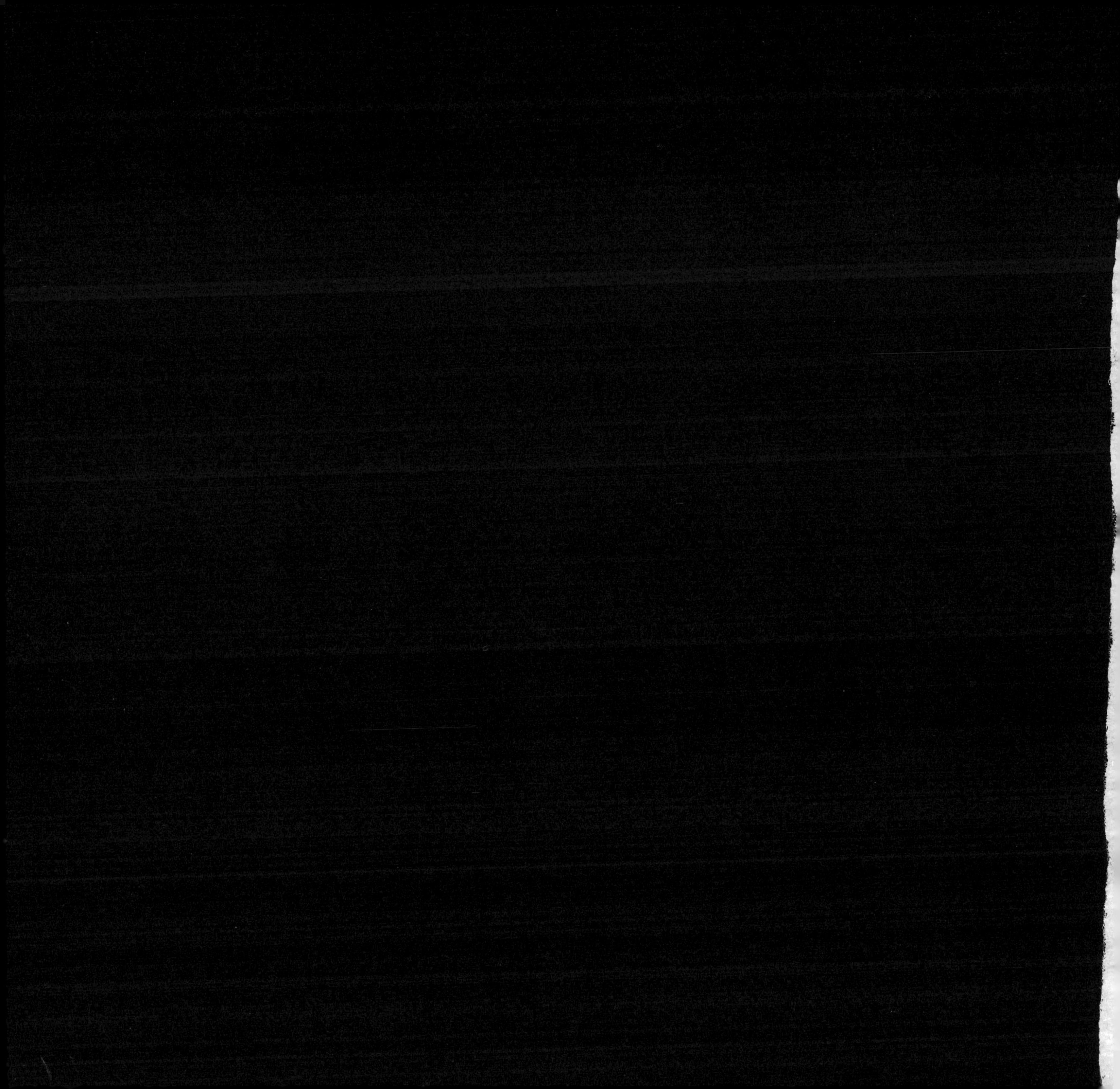

KYFFIN IN VENICE

First published in 2006 by
Gomer Press, Llandysul, Ceredigion SA44 4JL
www.gomer.co.uk

Second edition – 2006

ISBN 1 84323 664 8
ISBN-13 9781843236641
A CIP record for this title is available from the British Library

This book is published with the financial support of the
Welsh Books Council.

Printed and bound in Wales at
Gomer Press, Llandysul, Ceredigion

KYFFIN IN VENICE

KYFFIN WILLIAMS *in conversation with DAVID MEREDITH*

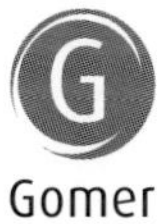

Gomer

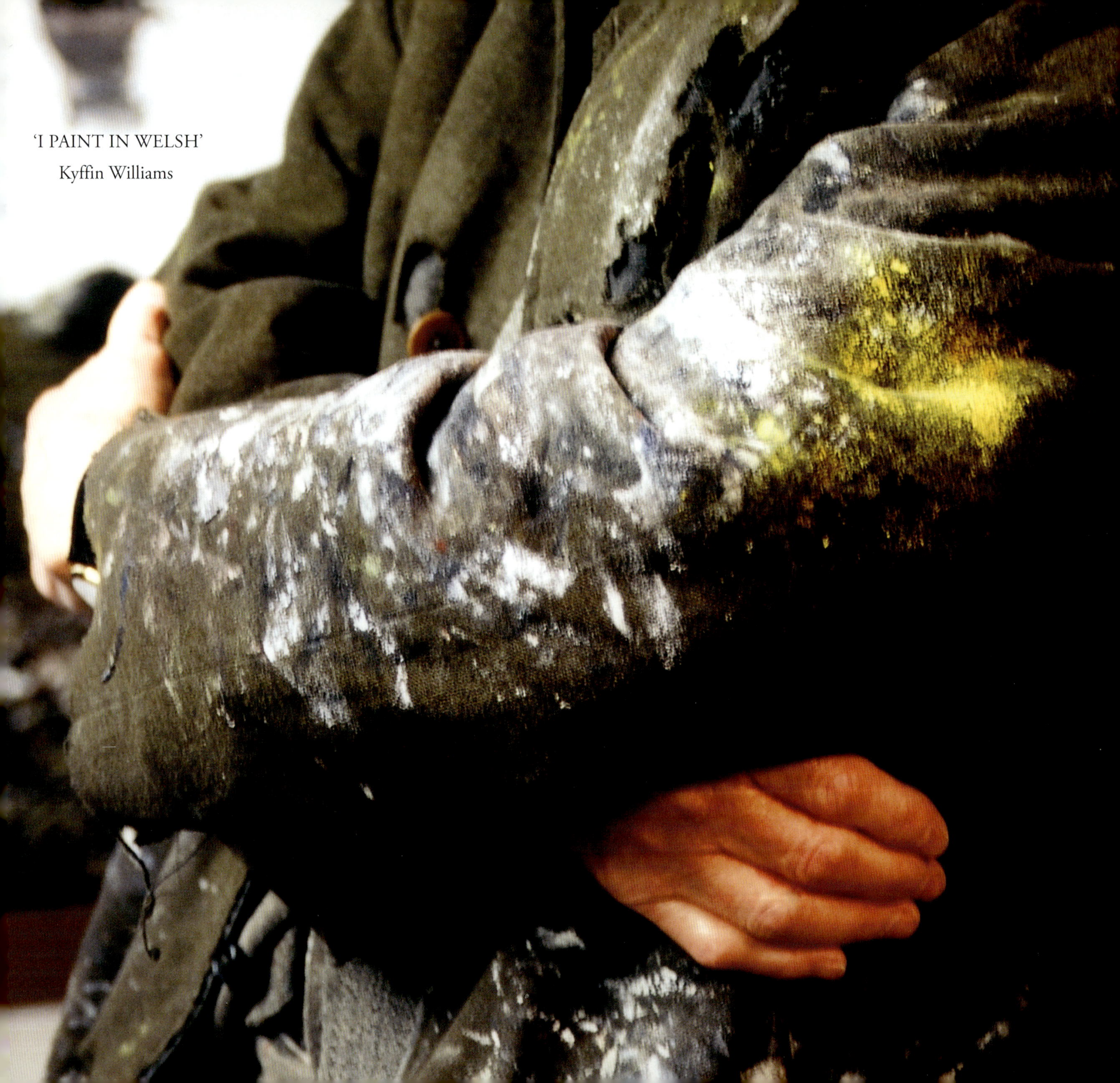
'I PAINT IN WELSH'
Kyffin Williams

INTRODUCTION BY SIR KYFFIN WILLIAMS, RA

It gives me great pleasure to write an introduction to this interview between David Meredith and myself. The 'casual conversation' began at my home, Pwllfanogl, Anglesey, and was filmed by Fflic Ltd. Following the interview, in preparation for the programme 'Reflections in a Gondola', commissioned by BBC Wales, we filmed at the BBC Cymru Wales studio in Bangor, at South Stack, Anglesey, in the area of 'Y Cnicht', in the Nanmor area, at the Royal Cambrian Academy Galleries, Conwy, at the National Library of Wales Aberystwyth and at Islawrdre, Dolgellau for Cader Idris. Later we set out on the great enterprise of filming in Venice where I ventured on the Grand Canal in a decorative gondola. I was very grateful for the sympathetic treatment I received from the whole crew: Gwenda Griffith, Producer; John Hefin, Director; Stephen Kingston, Cameraman; Steve Jones, Sound Recordist; Nia Jones, Production Assistant and David Meredith, Programme Consultant. Returning to the interview, there are so many questions in life and so few answers, but I hope the answers printed in these pages cast some light on my life and work.

KYFFIN WILLIAMS *March 2006*

It's a good game, you should try it; Kyffin Williams played it well. It's called 'Four Fortuitous Moments in my Life' – with as much emphasis as possible on 'fortuitous', i.e. chance, the unexpected, informal, lucky.

Normally it's the entries on the CV that seem to dictate our lives – school, college, posts held etc., but maybe, if we were honest, it's the huge small things that really directed our personal compass points, things that are never noted on a CV because they're personal, sometimes embarrassing and often time forgotten.

(I've played this game and was amazed at the four moments, e.g. had not my Uncle Llew by chance in 1950 seen a *Western Mail* advert inviting applicants to become BBC trainee production assistants in Cardiff I could well have lost an opportunity of a lifetime; one which gave me the lucky break, the passport, to fantastic experiences for the next 40 years. *Diolch* uncle Llew.)

Kyffin's four fortuitous moments were of course revealing and fascinating:

1. His birthplace in Anglesey – this chance dictated so much of the contents of his canvasses for the next 80 or so years.

2. A spiritual moment at the Ashmolean museum in Oxford while researching an art history essay. Seeing Piero Della Francesca's 'Resurrection' made him truly realise that painting was far more than reproduction; it involved love and obsession, themes that were to play a huge part in his life.

3. In 1947 and by now an art teacher at Highgate School in London he found himself

painting alone near Cader Idris. Having completed two canvasses, he clambered back down the mountain laden with paints, easel and palette, looking not unlike Thomas Rowlandson's famous 1799 aquatint of 'The Artist in Wales', to the house where he was lodging. On considering his day's labours in a critical manner, he sensed for the first time 'maybe, just maybe, I could make a living by painting'. Mercifully that intensely private and unexpected realisation became a reality and despite many hardships, Kyffin has managed to earn his keep by exercising his great love.

4. Venice. This much-painted lagoon city was the fourth choice. Why? Family connections (one of his forefathers made a fortune from mining copper at Parys Mountain in Anglesey and had houses in Berkley Square and Venice); the ever-present water; and the extraordinary pearly light. On reflection it was touch and go whether or not the fourth choice was to be Patagonia, as a chance Churchill Scholarship enabled him to spend some of the happiest days of his life amongst his fellow countrymen there. Shooting Kyffin in his gondola, sketching as he glided up the Grand Canal, was a joy. Any one of the crew will bend your ear with praise. His 'Reflections in a Gondola' will remain a treasured memory for us all.

If you want to learn more about his amazing life, read his wonderful autobiographies, *Across the Straits* and *A Wider Sky*. All I can add is to tell you another of my fortuitous moments. You've probably guessed it – the sublime pleasure of being in the company of a truly good and great man called Sir John Kyffin Williams RA. *Diolch* Kyffin.

For Sir Kyffin Williams RA 'the six-crempog boy'

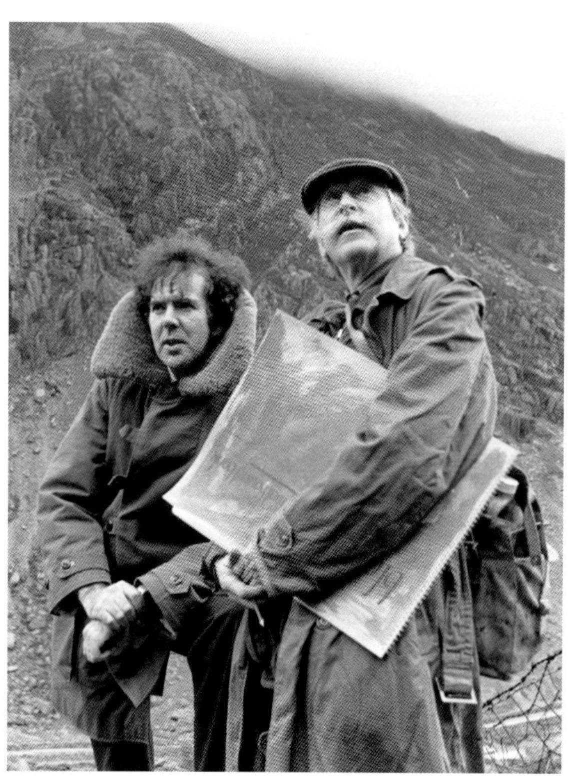

David Meredith and Kyffin at Nant Peris, Gwynedd,
filming the television programme, *Artists*, 1978

AN ARTIST ABROAD DAVID MEREDITH

I respect and admire Kyffin Williams, his humour, his inquiring mind, his love of the rocks, the fauna, the mountains and, above all, the people of Wales. People are paramount to him. His John Jones, the gaberdine-clad farmer, with binder cord as a belt, portrayed so many times, is no caricature: Kyffin knows and admires John Jones. He has walked and talked with him so many times over the years, he knows his mindset, representing as he does those farmers of Wales who have cared for their animals and land with equal love and attention.

It's July in the early 1970s; on behalf of HTV, the independent television company for Wales, I had invited Kyffin to judge an art competition. He immediately agreed. That day in July, I was Kyffin's assistant, carrying over 500 paintings here and there as Kyffin decided who was 'in' and who was 'out'. He worked tirelessly until the work was completed.

It was also early in the 1970s that I first saw Kyffin's Patagonian paintings: flowers, birds, horses, the Andes and the people of the Welsh community with such a heroic tale to tell. It can be a great source of pride for us all that the remarkable collection is housed and cared for at the National Library of Wales in Aberystwyth, bequeathed as a gift to the nation by the artist himself.

It's 1975 and I'm on the steps of the Royal Academy in London. Totally by accident, I meet Kyffin Williams, Royal Academican. As we put the world to order, Kyffin introduces me to the President of the Royal Academy, Sir Hugh Casson. We stood there in the London sunshine discussing the paintings of Tunnicliffe, galleries in Anglesey, and the world!

Now it's the late seventies, at Kyffin's home in Pwllfanogl, Anglesey. I'm in the presence of two great creative forces, two great men, the sculptor Ivor Roberts Jones and Kyffin himself. Ivor, whose father came from Aberystwyth, my home town, was responsible for the majestic sculpture of Winston Churchill in Westminster, London. Kyffin was vitally involved in this bronze sculpture, standing in as Churchill for Ivor in an old grey army coat. Ivor's masterly sculptures are numerous – of subjects ranging from opera singers to generals, politicians and actors to great literary figures. Kyffin has spent a lifetime promoting the artistic endeavours of Wales in all its many forms.

I'm at home at Ty'n Fedw Farm, Llanuwchllyn in the 1980s. Kyffin has joined the family for lunch. Also at the table is my mother's youngest brother, Seimon Lewis Jones, farmer of Tanybwlch Farm. Kyffin is very much at home – Seimon Lewis is a true blue 'John Jones'. After lunch, Kyffin goes to sketch the slopes of the Cynllwyd Valley. According to his own testimony, he is very fond of Merioneth. I note that his painting of Cader Idris, one of the county's most dramatic mountains, was painted as early as 1947.

1987, it's Kyffin retrospective exhibition at the National Museum of Wales, Cardiff. HTV is sponsoring the event alongside Barclays Bank and, as Head of Public Affairs for HTV,

I'm deeply involved. The cream of Welsh society is at the National Museum of Wales for this brilliant and exciting exhibition. One hundred and thirty-two paintings and drawings, amongst them some of the best portraits ever drawn. The Secretary of State for Wales, Nicholas Edwards, opens the exhibition. We all pay tribute to the genius of John Kyffin Williams. The exhibition would later tour to different parts of Wales.

Kyffin and I are walking up the slopes of Nant Peris, where I'm presenting a television programme on Kyffin, in a series on the artists of Wales. Kyffin is sketching one of his best-loved waterfalls, Cwm Glas, where the waters of Eryri cascade dramatically down the mountainside over huge boulders. Kyffin stands with one foot forward, the large sketchpad resting against his body. He is completely at home in the elements. Ignoring the camera, he concentrates totally on the waterfall; his eyes dart constantly from water to rocks to sketchpad. Using just a pencil, the waterfall is transferred as if by magic to the white sheet of paper. Not losing a minute, Kyffin proceeds to colour the finished artwork with shades of grey and black. I stand, looking on in amazement and admiration. Later, we visit the beach at Llanddwyn, Anglesey, where Kyffin, standing dramatically between two rocks, prepares initial sketches for one of his large seascapes.

May 2004, I'm at Kyffin's home, Pwllfanogl, Anglesey. Kyffin's travelling case, paints and bottle of water – for painting, not drinking – and one 20" x 16" sketchpad are ready to be packed into the BMW. We're off to Manchester Airport for our flight to Venice for the production of a lifetime, Kyffin Williams sketching and painting in Venice, Kyffin Williams in a gondola!

During that memorable flight, we discuss every topic under the sun: mapmaking in the Alps before the age of flight, the colour of the Dolomites, the fertility of the Po Valley and the genius of Van Gogh. This venture for me is a notable culmination of many artistic exploits with one of the great men of Wales.

Under the direction of my lifelong friend and collaborator John Hefin, I had the privilege of interviewing my hero and friend, Kyffin, on the hearth at Pwllfanogl, on the Menai Strait and to continue the conversation at the Danieli Hotel, Venice. The Venetian dream had begun when John and I met to discuss matters over tea and toast at Tynycornel Hotel, Talyllyn, Gwynedd. Producer Gwenda Griffith realised our dream with her usual tenacity.

During my conversation with Kyffin he avoided no questions, looked me straight in the eye and spoke with clarity, wit and humility – a great man, the greatest of artists. Wales can be proud of him.

KYFFIN WILLIAMS IN CONVERSATION WITH DAVID MEREDITH

DM Kyffin, people say that you are Wales' greatest artist, and I agree. You have painted our people, the mountains, the valleys, the animals of Wales, rivers, waterfalls. But is there one image more than another that inspires you, that drives you?

KW Well, when I was in London, away from Wales, I would think back to Wales and the image that did come to me then was invariably a lonely farmer on the mountain. When I think about it, I think that is probably it, the abiding image of north Wales when I'm away from Wales.

DM And yet that farmer today has become a driver of huge gleaming tractors, and some even spend holidays abroad golfing in Spain!

KW *'Aros mae'r mynyddau mawr'.*

DM So that image has remained with you?

KW It has, and the amazing thing is, no longer do the farmers wear sacks over their

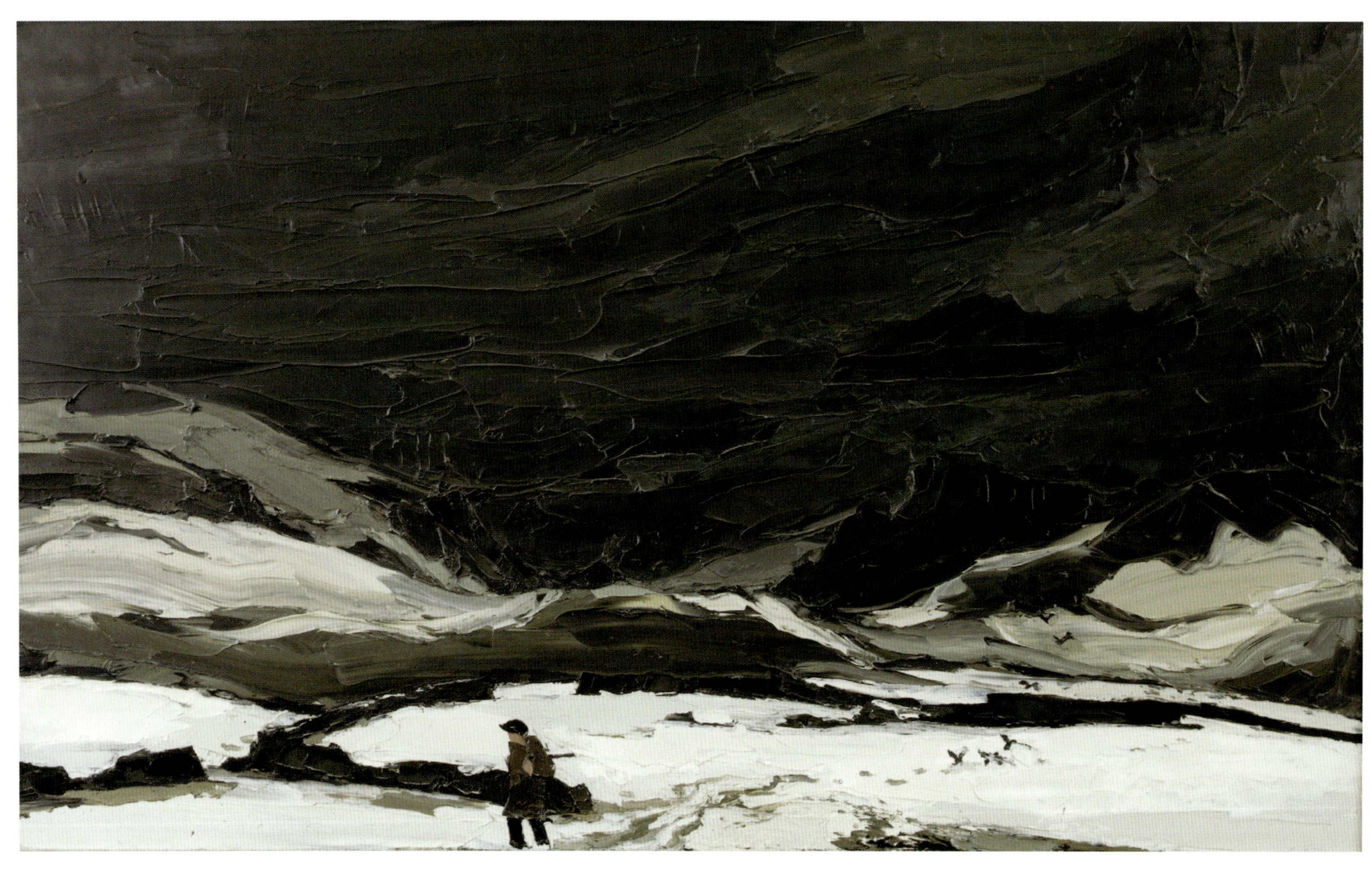

Farmer, Pontllyfni, 1971

shoulders, they wear anoraks and they are different. I suppose they won't exist in 200 years time – there won't be such a thing as a hill farmer, in less than a 100 years' time.

DM   That would be a frightening thought.

KW   Well, something will have gone. The sheep will be gone but the trees will come back and there will be a changed landscape. Maybe I have recorded something of that time before the change.

DM   I'm intrigued to know how on earth you have sustained your position in the art world with such style – I mean, you're a one man artistic power house! How have you been successful for such a long time?

KW   I suppose it's to do with the fact of obsession. I don't go around saying how wonderful Wales is and how wonderful the Welsh people are, but I think, being Welsh, there's some innate feeling which is underneath but never comes out except, possibly, in my paintings. I suppose I wanted to do it. I went to the Slade to study art but I didn't know what I was going to do really. But once I found it, it was absolutely obvious what I had to do – and I had to do what I knew best. That was the people of Gwynedd, the landscapes of Gwynedd,

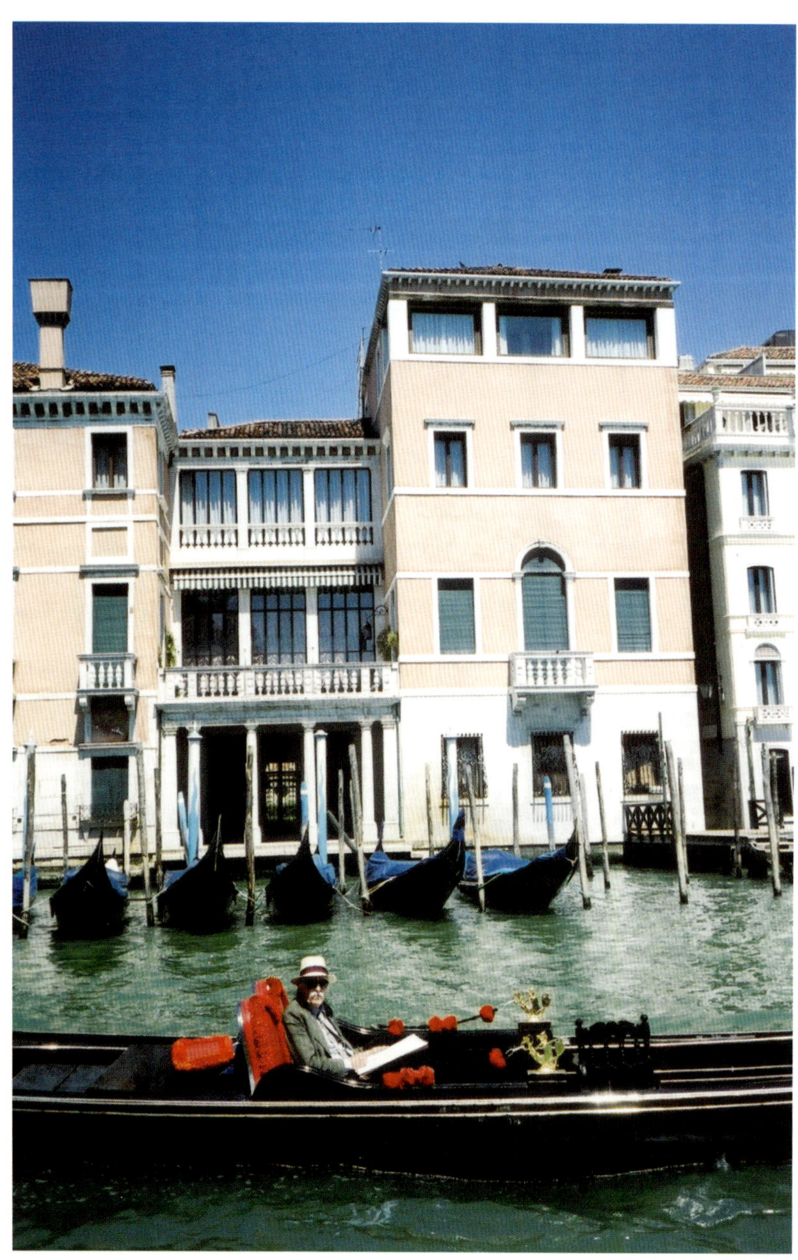

16   Kyffin on the Grand Canal

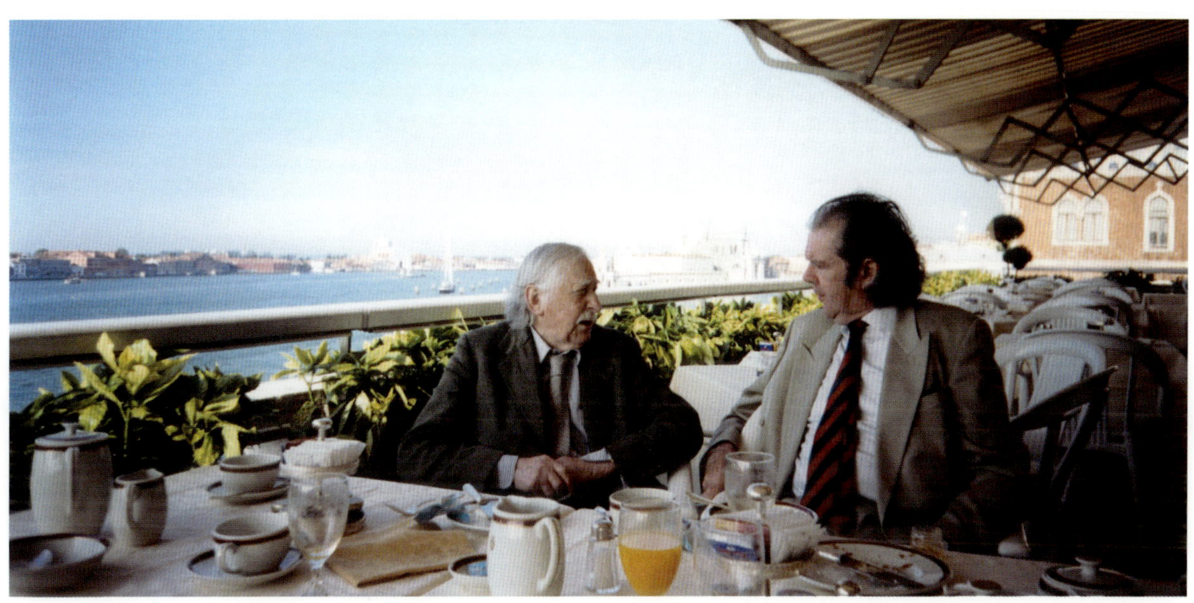

Kyffin and David Meredith chat over breakfast at Terrazza Danieli, the restaurant overlooking St Marks basin and the Lagoon, Venice

17

as I knew it, as my family had always known it, and some of my family had been painters too. There was the question of what subject matter should I have. Should I have the question of subtlety of light or should I have abstraction of things? It never occurred to me that it was absolutely simple, because really I was born without any talent and I had to take up art for the good of my health.

DM I can't accept that . . .

KW Well I had really no talent, I mean I wouldn't have got into the Slade had there not been a war because I really wasn't good enough.

DM You're a modest man.

KW No I'm not a modest man. I'm honest, I hope, but not modest. But what I did have, I came to realise, was far more important, and that was obsession for where I came from. It wasn't me going round starry-eyed saying 'I've got an obsession, I've got an obsession'; it's something that's deep down. Most people have it, I think. So that is why I painted, and I suppose that to be obsessive is far more important than to have talent. Talent is a facile thing; it's something that's done easily, and therefore there's little depth in it. Obsession means you feel deeply about something; sometimes it's about something that's not worthwhile, and then you're barmy. Quite close to barmy is an obsession.

DM Genius, is that a close relative as well?

KW Oh yes, very close together. Anyhow, it's that obsession, you see, because if you're obsessed, you do in fact create your own talent because you want to do something enough. If one is just talented, it's very rare that people become obsessive. It would be nice if you could. But I didn't have any talent at all. I mean my early life drawings at the Slade were absolutely pathetic. But there we are, I was there. I managed to do it. I taught myself to draw really and it was an act of communication. I painted – and I still do paint – entirely for myself. But I'm able to communicate purely because I am obsessed and I love what I do; only by that can you communicate with people. If you have no love for anything, you cannot communicate – at least I don't think you can.

DM Is it the teacher in you that also drives you forward, this wish to give knowledge to others?

KW Well, I certainly would have liked to have taught in an art school but no art school

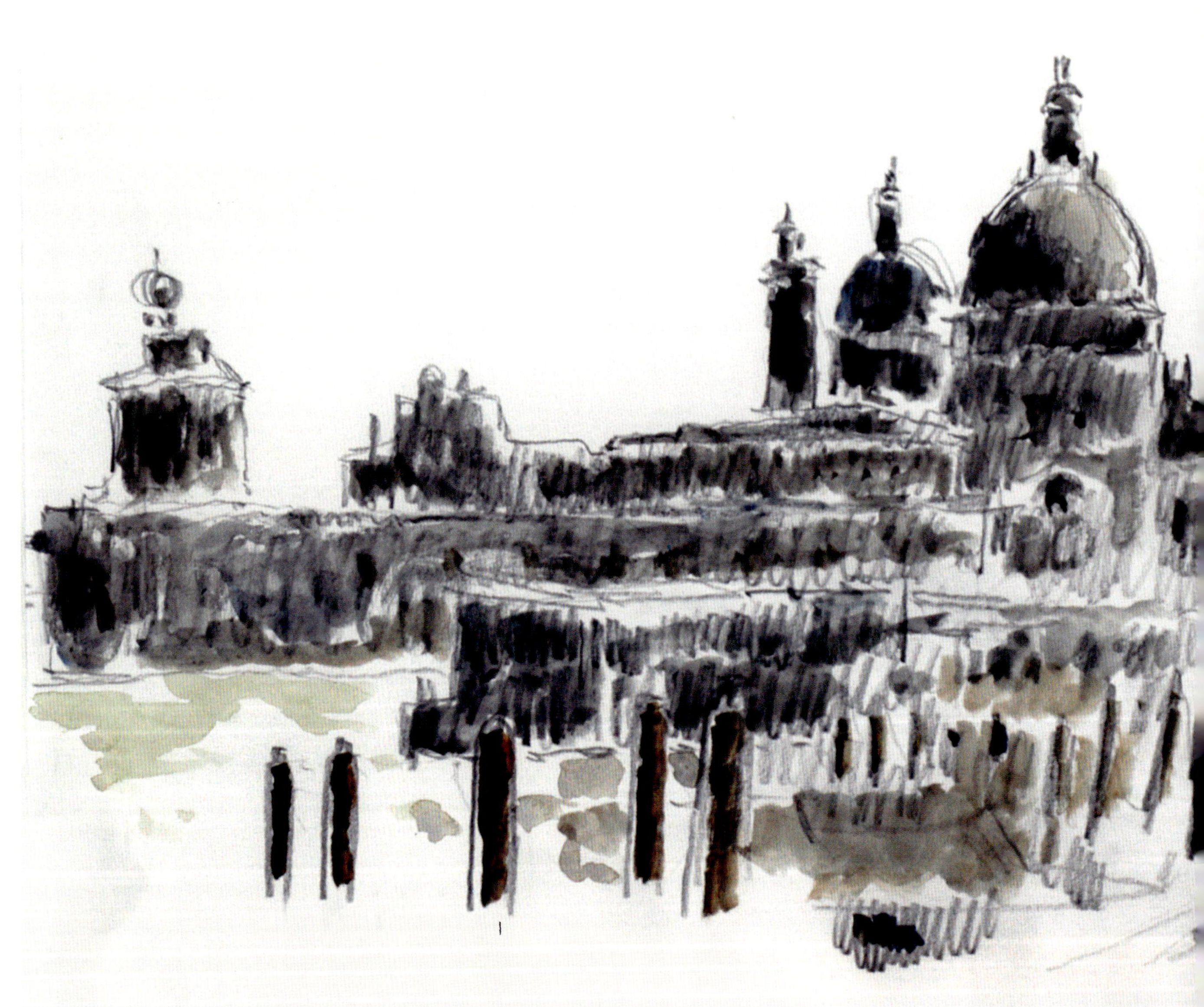

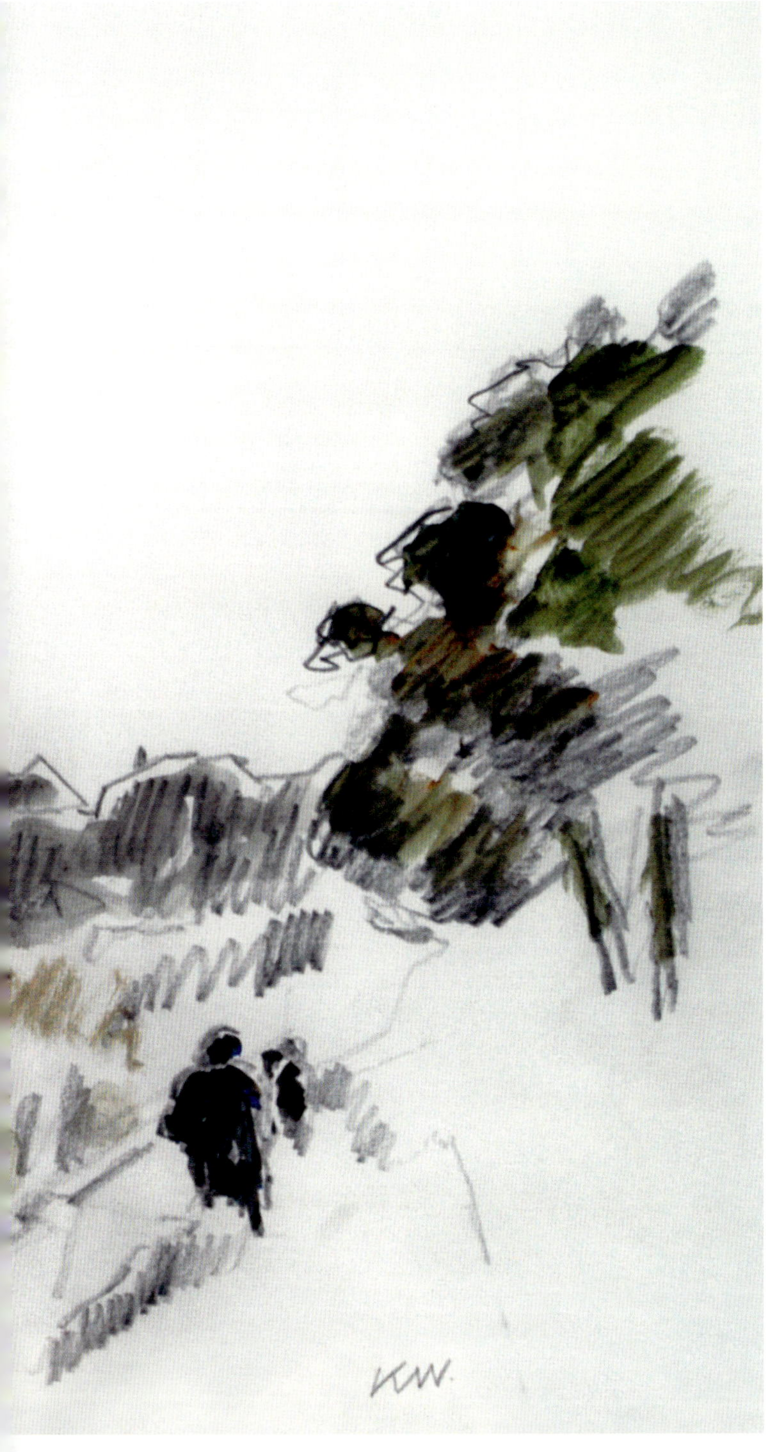

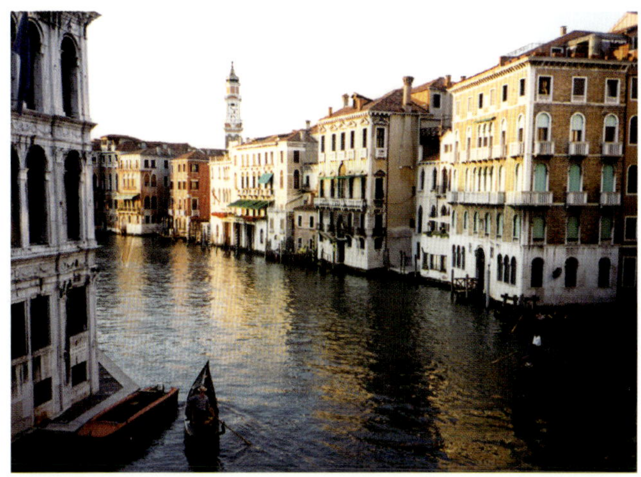

Shadows on the canal

The church of Santa Maria della Salute with the Customs House, 2004

would have me! I think my ideas about art were quite contrary to the art schools in London. They were all trying to move forward into the new world of art which denied any love in art at all and, to me, it was an anathema really. So I was unable to teach there. I always wanted to teach mature students but I never could so I taught in a boys' school. I was very lucky because art schools can be pretty average artistic cesspools really – they really are terrible. They manipulate the students and don't even bother to teach them. And that's been the downfall of British art ever since the War. I was very lucky. I realised actually that I was lucky. I was more or less my own boss and I could do my own thing. I had the school holidays which meant I was able to go back to Wales and charge my batteries and do a lot of drawings from which I could paint when I went back to London.

DM   What part of Wales was that, when you say you went back?

KW   Well, we stayed in south Caernarfonshire. I didn't paint so much in south Caernarfonshire; I was in the mountains. I was very lucky you know to start hunting a lot with the farmers after foxes in the mountains, and the fox took me to places people don't normally go and I saw then the mountains and Gwynedd in all weathers.

DM   I see now, I understand how you can paint foxes and dogs with such exactness, so brilliantly.

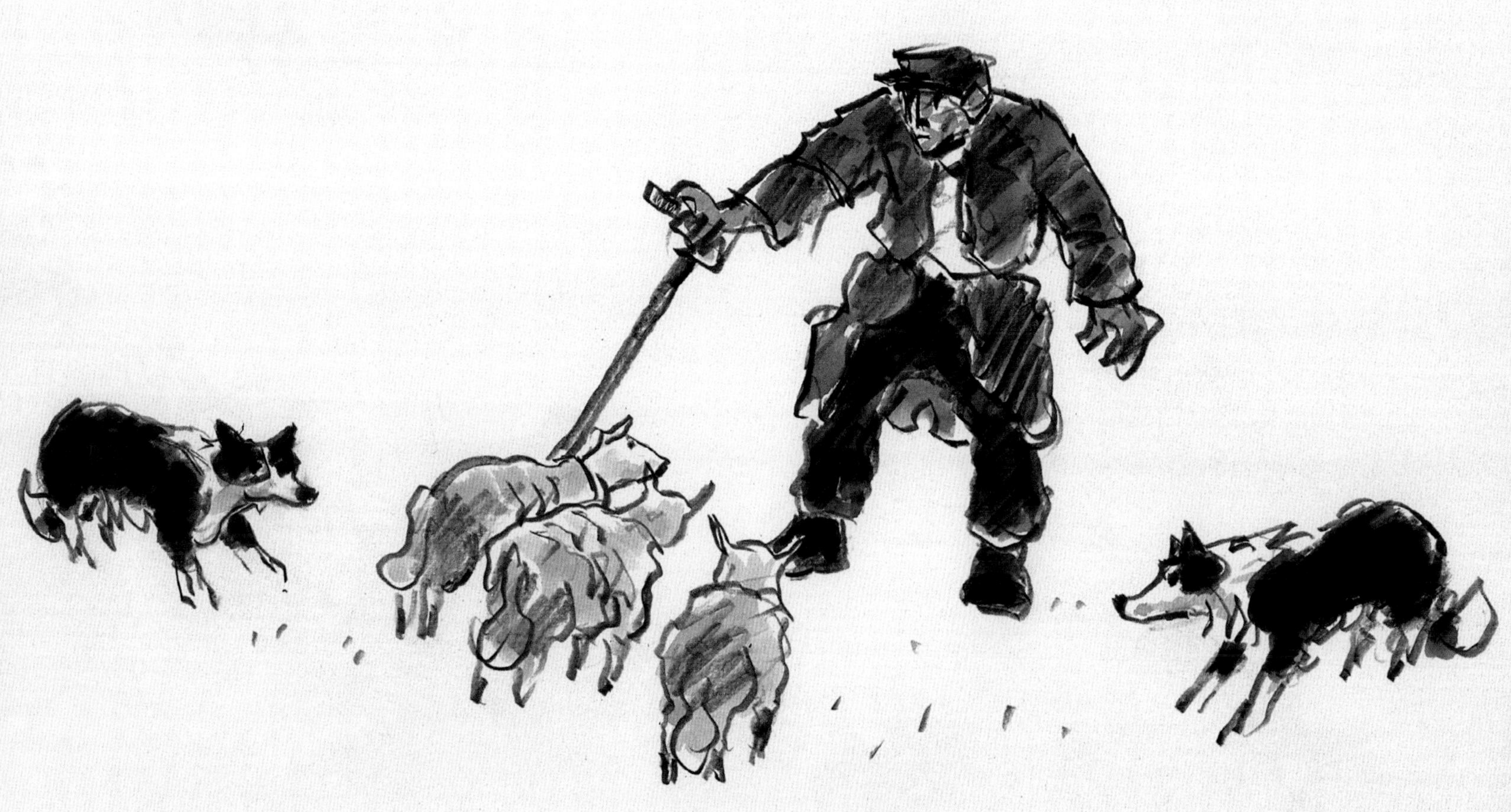

Farmer with sheep, 1998

KW   Oh I don't know, I don't know if I can. But amongst my best paintings I think is a fox; I'd gone hunting near Llanfrothen. It was a terribly bad scenting day and the fox knew it. The fox was walking along in front of the hounds, trying to pick up his scent, and casually stopping, looking back, to see how close they were. He jumped up onto a rock and sat on top of the rock with his head between his paws and I saw it there and I put it down on a bit of paper and after a bit the hounds came rather closer and he just shot off and sauntered away.

DM   I think your painting of the sheepdog, with what a Welsh poet called that *'untroed oediog'*, that hesitant foot, if that is the correct translation, is brilliant.

KW   Well, they are wonderful things, sheepdogs, somehow. I love the way he's tied as if by a bit of elastic to his master and he does something, off he goes and suddenly there's a whistle or a shout and he stops; he's held back by the bit of elastic. There's always that relationship between the farmer and the dog.

DM   I'm thinking about a farmer shouting at his dog; you know, that's how people speak, well not quite as they would with a child, but there's something quite human about it.

KW   Well, yes, there is. And another thing, perhaps I've got to admit it: a black and white dog is very attractive on the mountain and I love the contrast of dark and light. That sums up the mountains to me – the farmer, a lonely farmer, a stick and a dog.

DM   Your formative years, the early period of your childhood between, say, one and ten years old, were they happy years?

KW   Well yes, my childhood was a happy one. I can't remember any difference of opinion between my father and my mother. It was a well-ordered household. My father was a very warm, affectionate person. My mother basically was a very affectionate person but she did not think it to be right ever to be affectionate. So I was brought up without any cuddling or kisses or anything like that. It was very sad for my mother; she just could not do it. She felt it wrong to do it – I don't know why this was. She worshipped her father, I think. But I did have security, even though I didn't have affection from her. I had affection from my father. My father was very good really; one thing he did not ever draw back on was books. If ever we wanted a book, we'd get it. And he'd take us down to Smiths in Porthmadog in order to buy a book and my brother, who was far more clever than I was – he was a brilliant scholar – he always bought a high-flying book and I always bought a book on birds or something. But he was terribly keen on us having books.

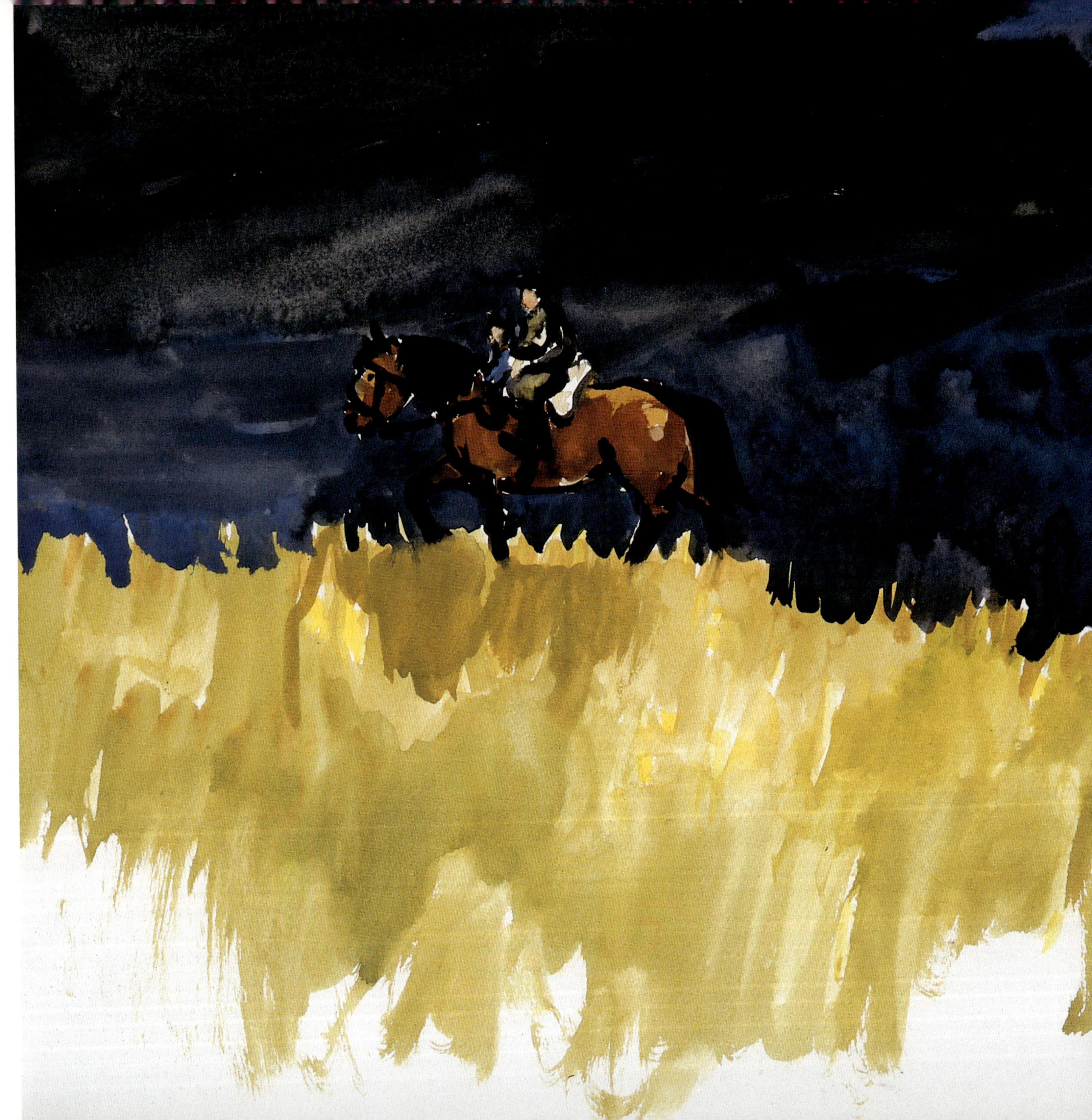

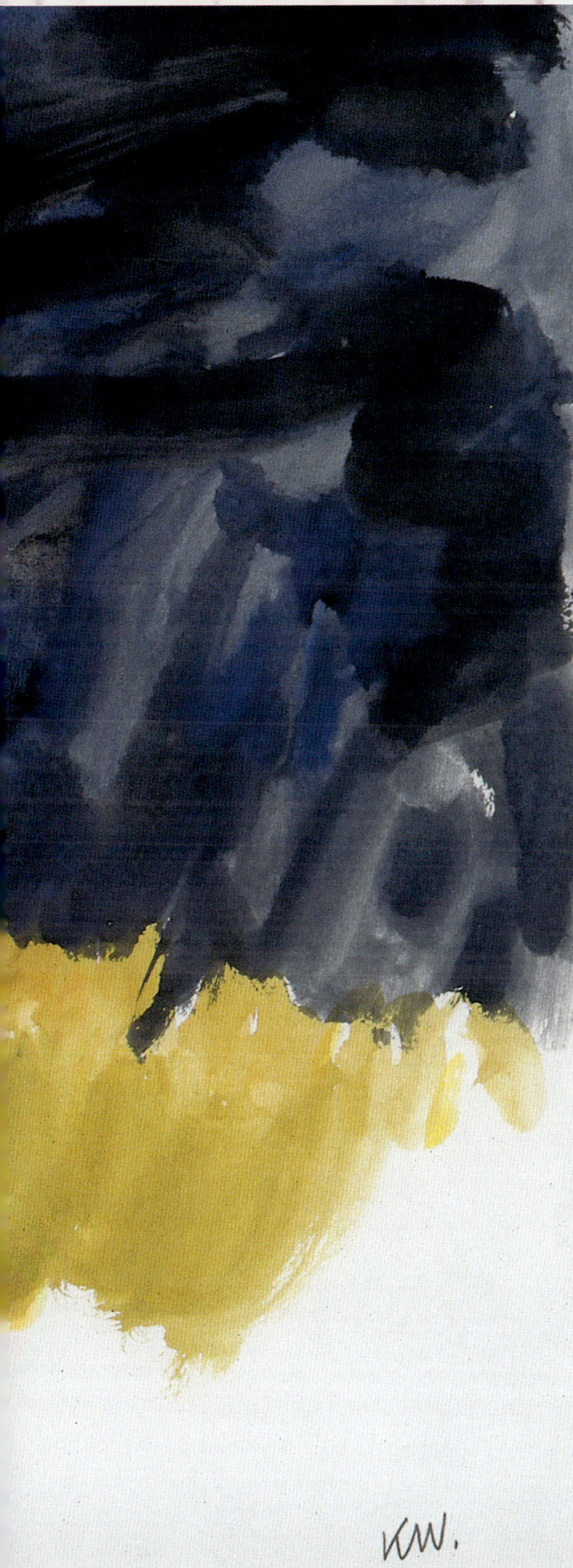

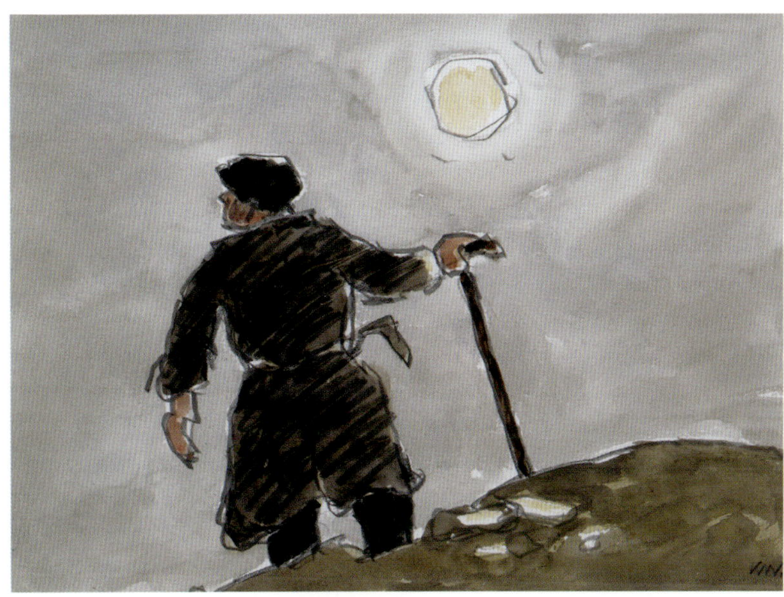

Farmer and Sun, 1997

Rider and son, Patagonia, 1969

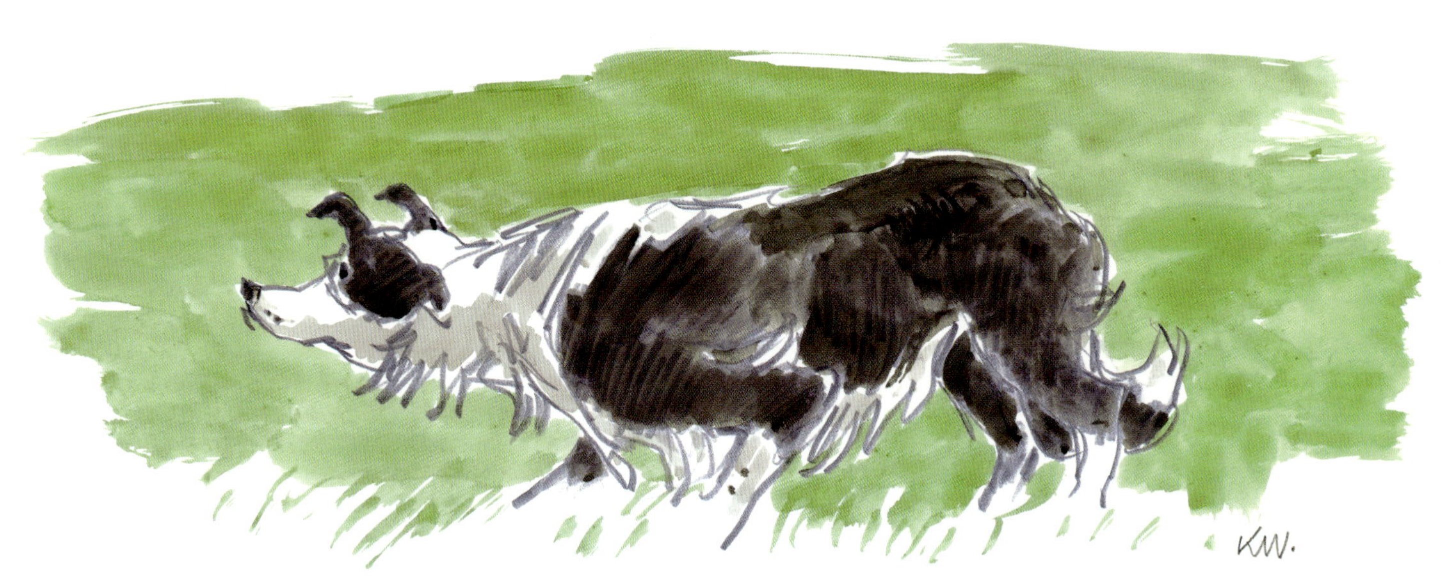

28   Mot the sheepdog, 1988

DM Was your brother older than you?

KW He was older than I was, yes. He was better than me at everything, which was a very good thing really. He was better in work; he was a scholar in Shrewsbury; he was captain of rugby at Shrewsbury; he was good at games; he was a swell.

DM Likewise, my brother beat me at everything, be it cards, games, cricket, soccer, everything. For me it was a sickening feeling.

KW Well, I never resented it because he was obviously so much better than I was. It never worried me and he was always very kind to me. He never hit me or anything. I hit him once, and he just looked at me. No, more or less I think it was a happy childhood and my father, he loved people. Both my father and mother were fluent Welsh speakers. My mother wouldn't speak Welsh because she felt it was rather infra dig to speak Welsh but my father loved it. He got on terribly well with everybody.

DM Where was he from?

KW My father? He was a native of Anglesey. My family had lived in Anglesey since hundreds and hundreds of years. His father was born in Llanfair yng Nghornwy rectory. My great-grandfather was born in the old family home, Treffos in Llansadwrn, and my great-great-grandfather was born in Treffos in Llansadwrn too, it having been bought in about 1720 by my great-great-great-grandfather. I think it was a very happy family. The family gravestones are in the church at Llansadwrn; on my great-great-great-grandfather's it says 'of a kindly disposition' and on my great-great-great-great-great-grandfather's, the same thing – 'of a kindly disposition', so they were all very humorous people.

DM   In 1968–69 you visited Patagonia on a Churchill Foundation. Your collection of paintings of the landscape and the people, of the fauna and the animals in Patagonia is a remarkable collection. The paintings are, in my view, some of the greatest treasures of the National Library of Wales in Aberystwyth. Tell me about that experience in Patagonia.

KW It was a wonderful experience. I'd always wanted to go to Patagonia because, to me, it was a fantastic story – this transposing of these Welsh people from Wales to such a remote part of South America, and they were so determined to carry on with the Welsh language and the Welsh way of life miles away from home. I wanted to meet all the Welsh people there so far away from home and when I got there I found that there was no *hiraeth*, which

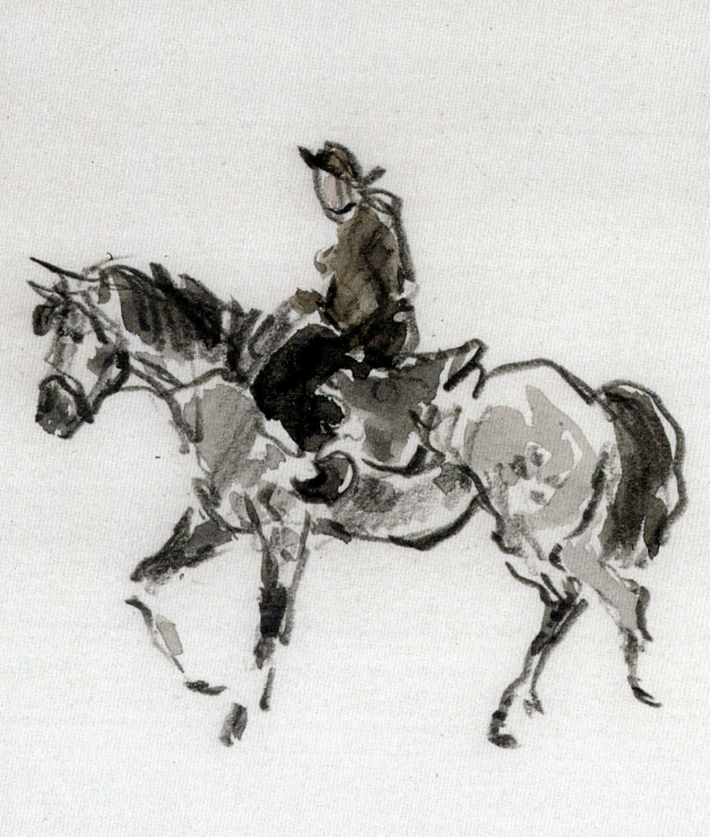
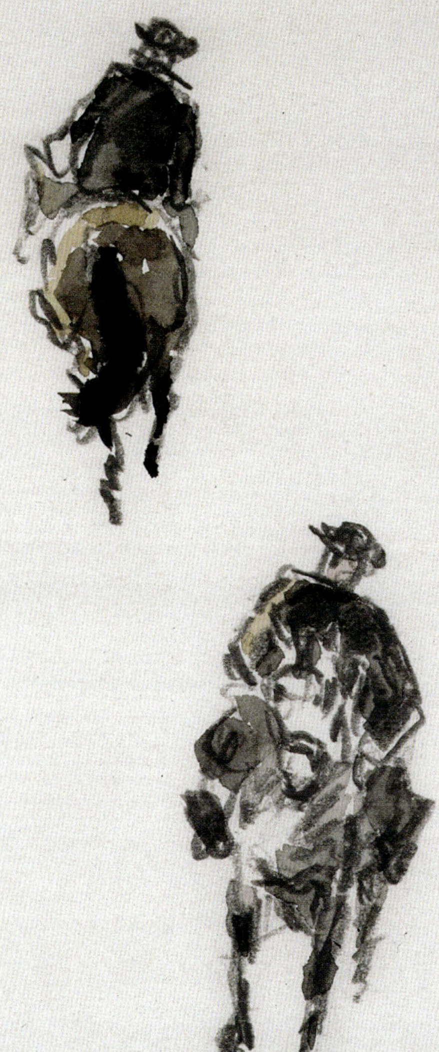

Riders above Esquel, 1969

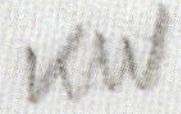

was interesting. They made their minds up and they were going to stick to it. Some of them said they'd probably made a mistake but they weren't going to leave – there was nothing better beyond the valley, of course, nothing but desert, really. So I decided to do a lot of drawing. I'd do the people, the birds, the animals, the flowers, the landscape in the lower valley and the valley in the Andes, Cwm Hyfryd. And I worked all the time; I had to work very hard, because there was no chance of coming back if I had forgotten something – I couldn't just get on a bus and go back!

DM   And you took a great many photographs during that visit?

KW   Yes. I'm not a photographer but I thought I ought to buy a camera to record what I saw. I remember every time I did a drawing I took a photograph of what I'd done and I had some 700 drawings in the end and 700 photographs! I was amazed when I came back how the photographs had come out. I gave my camera away then because I was afraid I would be taking photographs instead of drawing.

DM   But it is an amazing collection?

KW   Well I don't know, it is a record.

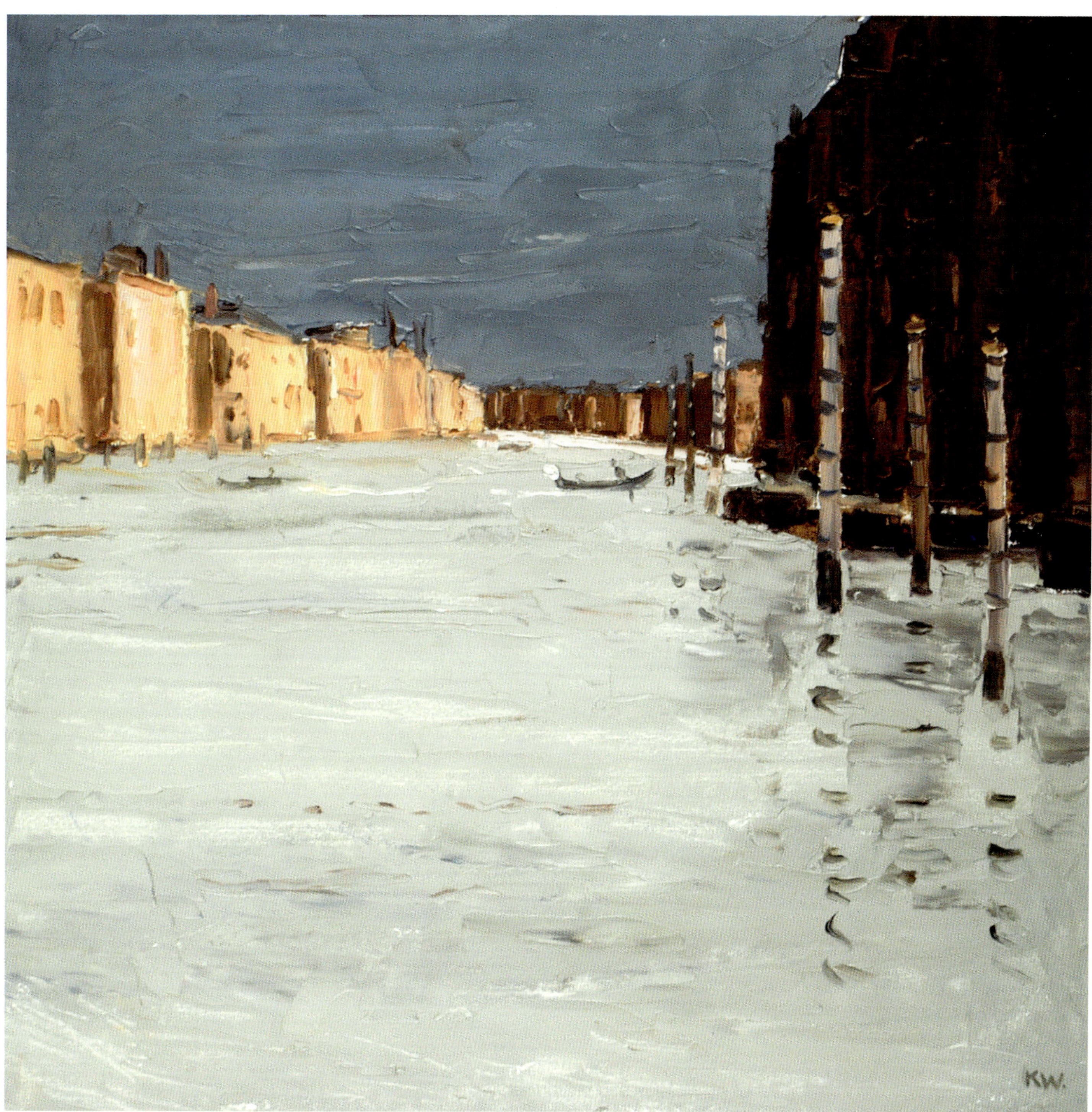

KW.

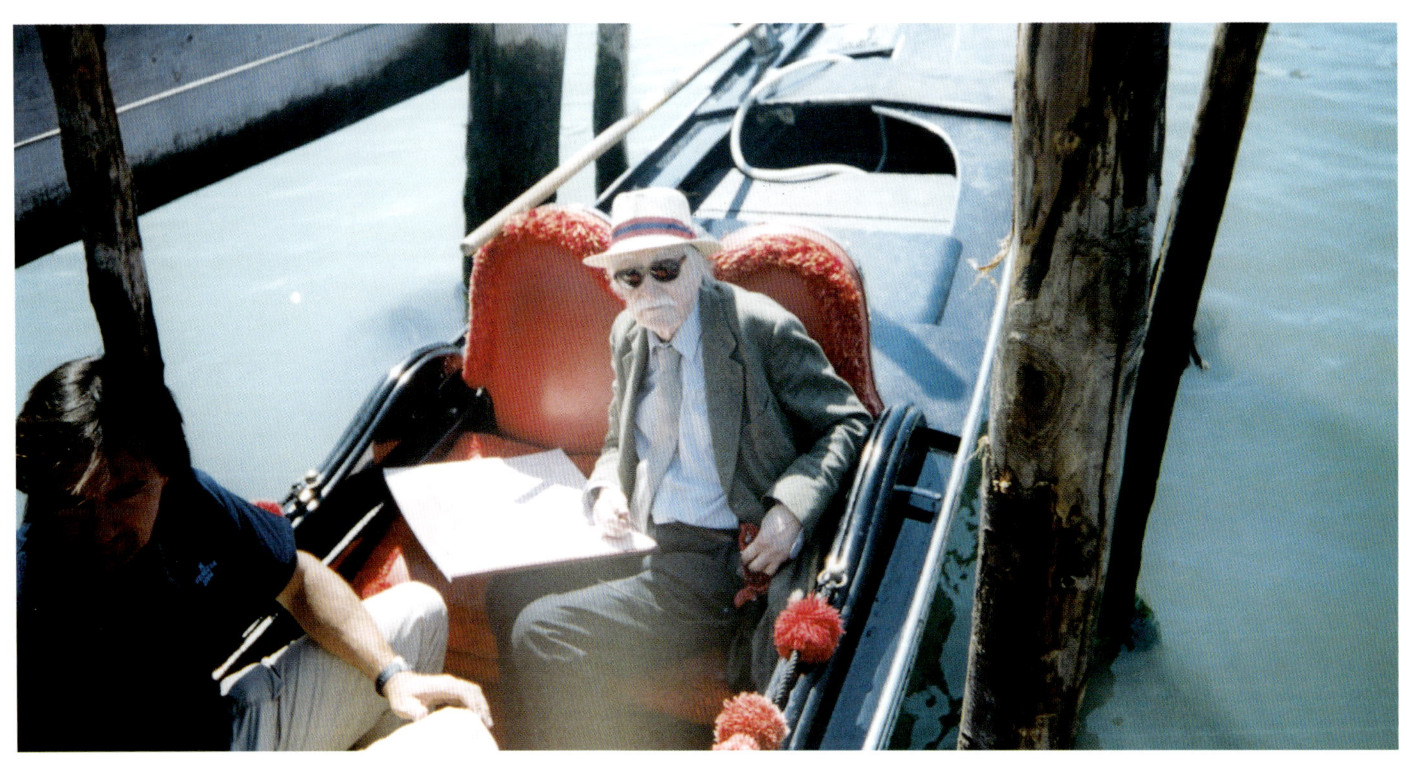

Kyffin prepares for a day of filmimg with Stephen Kingston

DM   I'm particularly fond of your pencil drawings in Patagonia.

KW Luckily, you see, I've always been fascinated by birds and animals, so I drew them and there's wonderful birdlife out there. Oddly enough, in the desert the birds were slightly yellowy, the flowers of the desert were yellowy and then there's a thing called an *ouraka* which is a sort of a yellowish Jay and the *benta veo* – and that was yellowish too! Then up in the Andes there's a tremendous number of kingfishers and hawks and there's a terrible bird in Dyffryn Camwy called *teru teru* – it's a spurred plover – and that's a fantastic bird. I was there at the time when they were having their young and they were very aggressive; they used to fly at you and, if they didn't like you, the humerus bone in their wing, a spur, shot out and they'd shoot past your head! I got totally fed up with them shouting *teru teru*, diving on me. And then when I went up to the Andes, there were eagles and condors up in Cwm Hyfryd.

DM   You went to Patagonia by boat. Why by boat?

KW   Well I had an idea that my Spanish was non-existent and that I'd meet some Spanish people on the boat who'd teach me. I did – I shared a cabin with a lecturer in English from the University of Buenos Aires, a fantastic gaucho called Luis Gonzales and a pastry cook

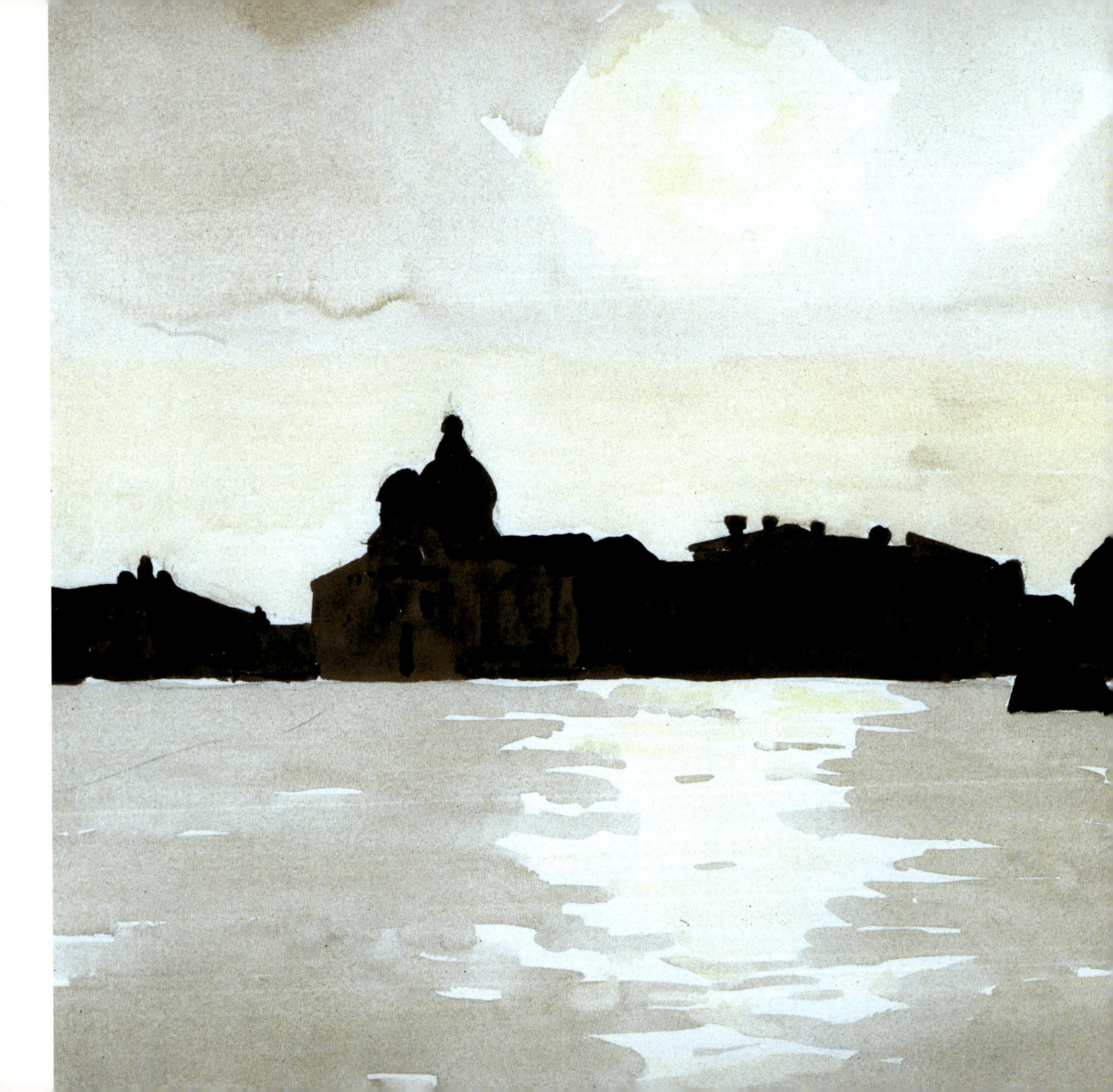

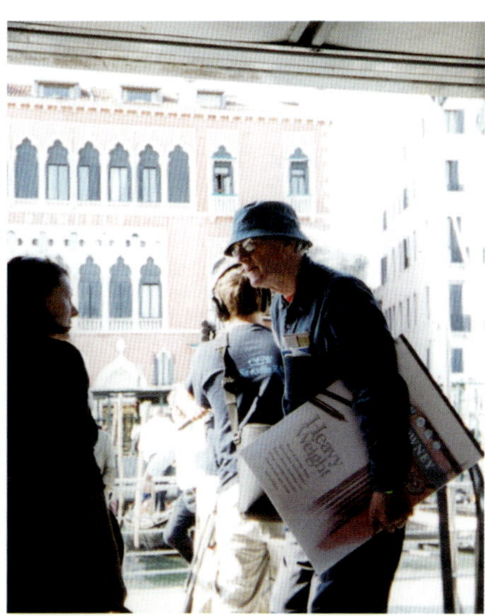

John Hefin and Gwenda Griffith disembarking from vaporetto

The Giudecca, Venice, 1979

from Montevideo called Gennaro Bastos, but they all spoke English to me, which wasn't much good! So I arrived in Buenos Aires without speaking any Spanish at all.

DM   And you have met, over the years, people that were in Patagonia when you were there, people who have come back to Wales on visits?

KW   Oh yes, they've been down here in Pwllfanogl. They say how much the condition of my road reminds them of Patagonia!

DM   You travelled on horseback in Patagonia?

KW   Oh yes. Luckily I could. They assumed that anybody from this country going down there would be able to ride; it's not so. But I had loved riding for some time and the first morning I was in the Andes, I woke up, and attached to my bedroom window was a horse. It was a horse for me – a pretty dreary old horse, but nevertheless it went. The first day I was there, I remember the old Senora Gwenonwy Berwyn de Jones wanted me to deliver a sack of onions to her son, Fred, who had a farm or a ranch up at the head of the valley, so this Indian boy saddled this horse for me and we had to cross the River Percy which was pretty well in flood. I thought I'd better let the horse do that and, of course, it did and

into a gallop and we galloped up Cwm Hyfryd. I got to the great entrance to the ranch and when I got off my horse I saw that the sack of the onions was limp. There was a hole in the bottom: every onion was spilt all the way back to Trefelin! So I had to go on the old plodder again and do a paper onion chase all the way back, getting off and picking up onion after onion . . .

DM You have been involved with drawing and painting for over 60 years. Is there one artist more than another that has influenced you or inspired you, and is artistic influence important?

KW Well, artistic influence is vital, I think, for any artist up to the age of 30 or 40. If, by then, you have not begun to find the influence by yourself, you will never be a painter. You use other artists for the best reasons and out of that, there should come your personality. That is what gives the mood in a painting and if you're still imitating after 40, you've had it, I think. In all the years up until you're 40, you should be finding yourself and using other artists in order to enable you to find yourself, and then after that, you really should be able to do your best work. In a way, artists who flourish very young, sometimes it's not a very good thing and, if they're too successful too young, its a great danger I think.

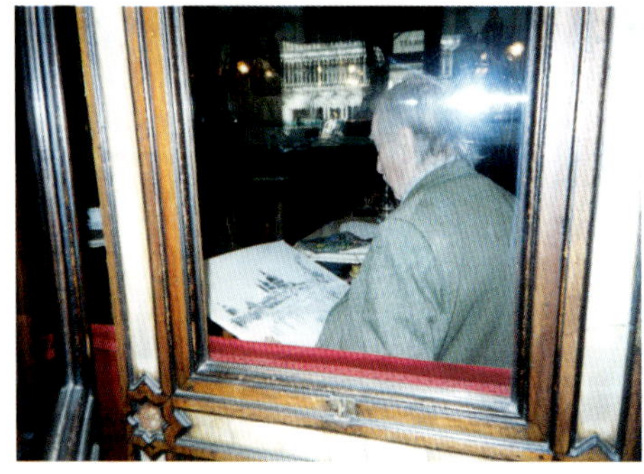

Kyffin sketching at Caffè Florian

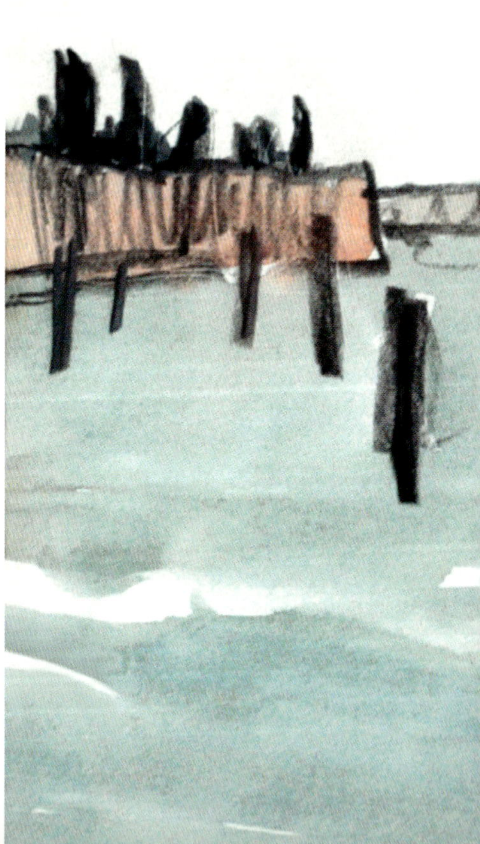

Warehouse on the Giudecca, 1979

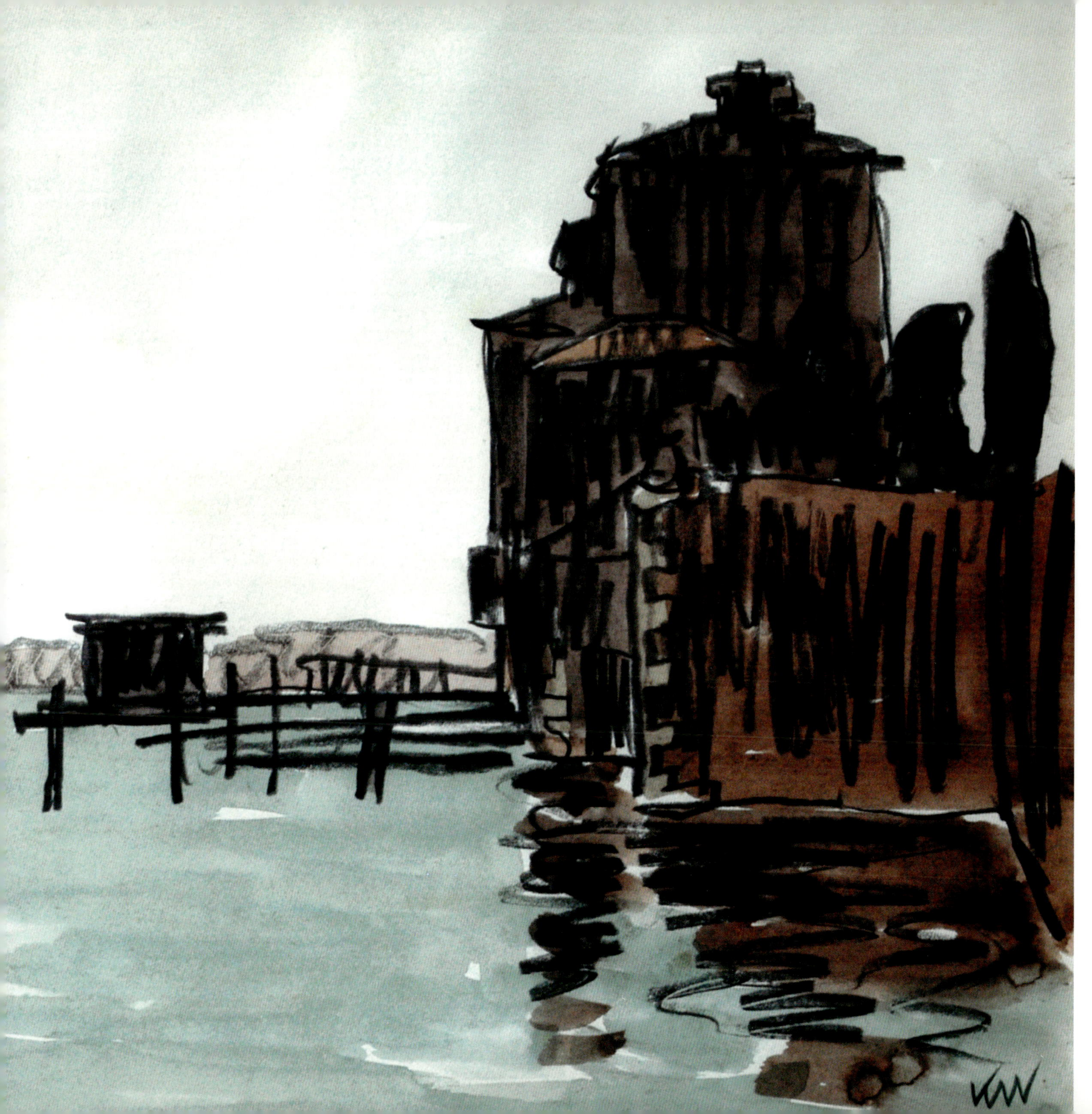

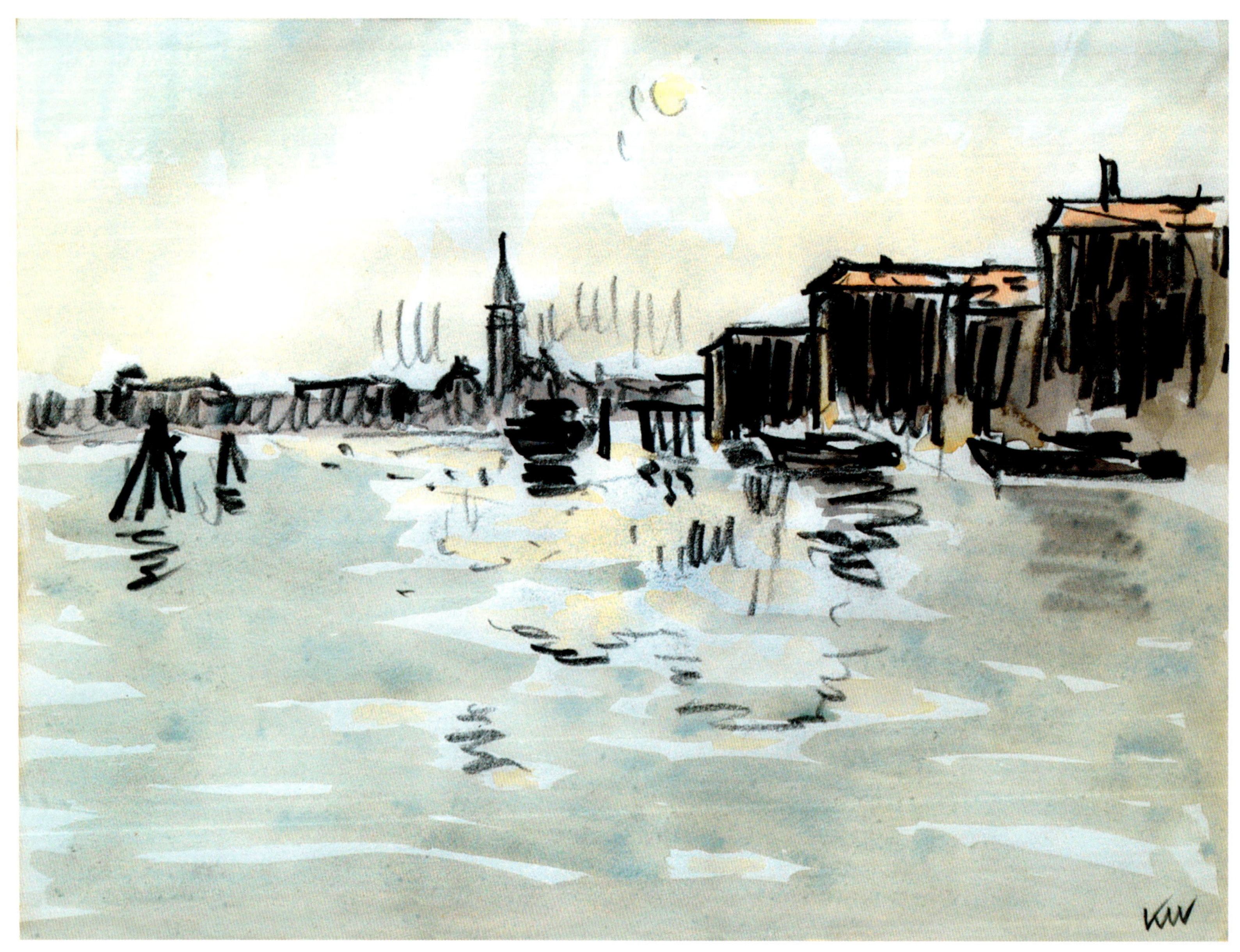

Boat off Murano, 1979

DM And in your period up to about 40, which particular artists would have influenced you?

KW Well I was a bit of an ass really; I went to an art school on doctor's orders, never took it seriously. I really thought that art was looking at something and putting it down. Suddenly, I saw a painting by Piero della Francesca in the Library of the Ashmolean Museum; it was 'The Resurrection of Christ'. It actually hit me, poleaxed me – the emotion in it and the mood, incredible mood, powerful, powerful mood. It made me weep when I saw it; tears just rolled down my cheeks – it was very embarrassing – and that was my 'road to Damascus', my conversion really, because I began to realise then that there's something spiritual which should come into painting – something which is almost entirely lacking today, which seems such a tragedy. In these old painters, there was a tremendous love of humanity as a spirit.

DM You emphasise mood. Do you regard mood in a painting as vital?

KW I don't like to say that it's vital to everyone but, to me, yes it's vital, it's emotion. I react to pictures that are emotional. They are my yardstick because they make me weep, you see. Some paintings by Rembrandt, they make me weep. That full spirit and love of a picture is being transferred to me. I won't go along and say 'that's clever' – which is a reaction people have to certain works – they mean nothing to me, those sort of paintings.

There are many artists whose works I love. Of course, I like Rembrandt. Rembrandt, I suppose, is the most loved artist in the world, because he had a passion for things and people. Of course, there's another artist who is certainly not one of the greatest artists who ever lived but is a most loved artist and that is Vincent van Gogh. He's the most popular artist in the world; he gets around into every bedsit of every art student in the world from Japan to San Francisco because he loved more deeply, it seems, than anybody else and was able to communicate that love. He wanted to communicate; he just had to paint his love of things, be it flowers or people or landscape, and that was it. He certainly wasn't the greatest artist who ever lived, but he was one of the most popular, if not *the* most popular.

DM Going back to Rembrandt; if I'm correct, Caravaggio had a great influence on Rembrandt's work. Has Caravaggio influenced you?

KW Well, he hasn't really. I mean he was a wonderful artist, there's no doubt about it. But he hasn't really influenced me because the people in his pictures are remote. There is a remoteness in Italian paintings and Caravaggio was one of the first Italian painters to reduce this element of remoteness; he brought the ordinary people in and that was a change. But with the artists from the Low Countries, you can go into their paintings and you can shake hands with some of the people in them. You wouldn't dare do that in an Italian painting – I mean, you could be an intruder! It's a totally different thing, so very often portraits by artists like Hans Memling are absolutely glorious. I saw a painting the other day, a reproduction of a painting, by Michael Sweerts, a seventeenth century artist. I hadn't actually heard of Michael Sweerts before, but this was an absolutely glorious portrait of a girl. It had at one time been considered to have been by Vermeer but then scholars decided it was not by Vermeer – but it was as good as a Vermeer. There are so many lovely paintings by slightly obscure people which really are very moving, but they're not consistent like some of the great masters, men like Rubens, Rembrandt and Franz Hals – they are able to produce character in people. El Greco could do it; some of his portraits are wonderful. Well, it's too big a subject to talk about.

DM You've given freely of your time to develop the arts centres of Wales: I'm thinking in particular about the Royal Cambrian Academy Galleries in Conwy where you're President; you've given succour and encouragement to young artists, you've been an ambassador for Wales, and yet the authorities in Wales are not heeding your call, and the call of others, to establish a proper museum of Welsh art. Is this disappointing to you?

KW Oh, it's very disappointing. I've always wanted a gallery for Welsh art because I believe that we, the people of Wales, are a culturally unbalanced nation. We love our poetry, music

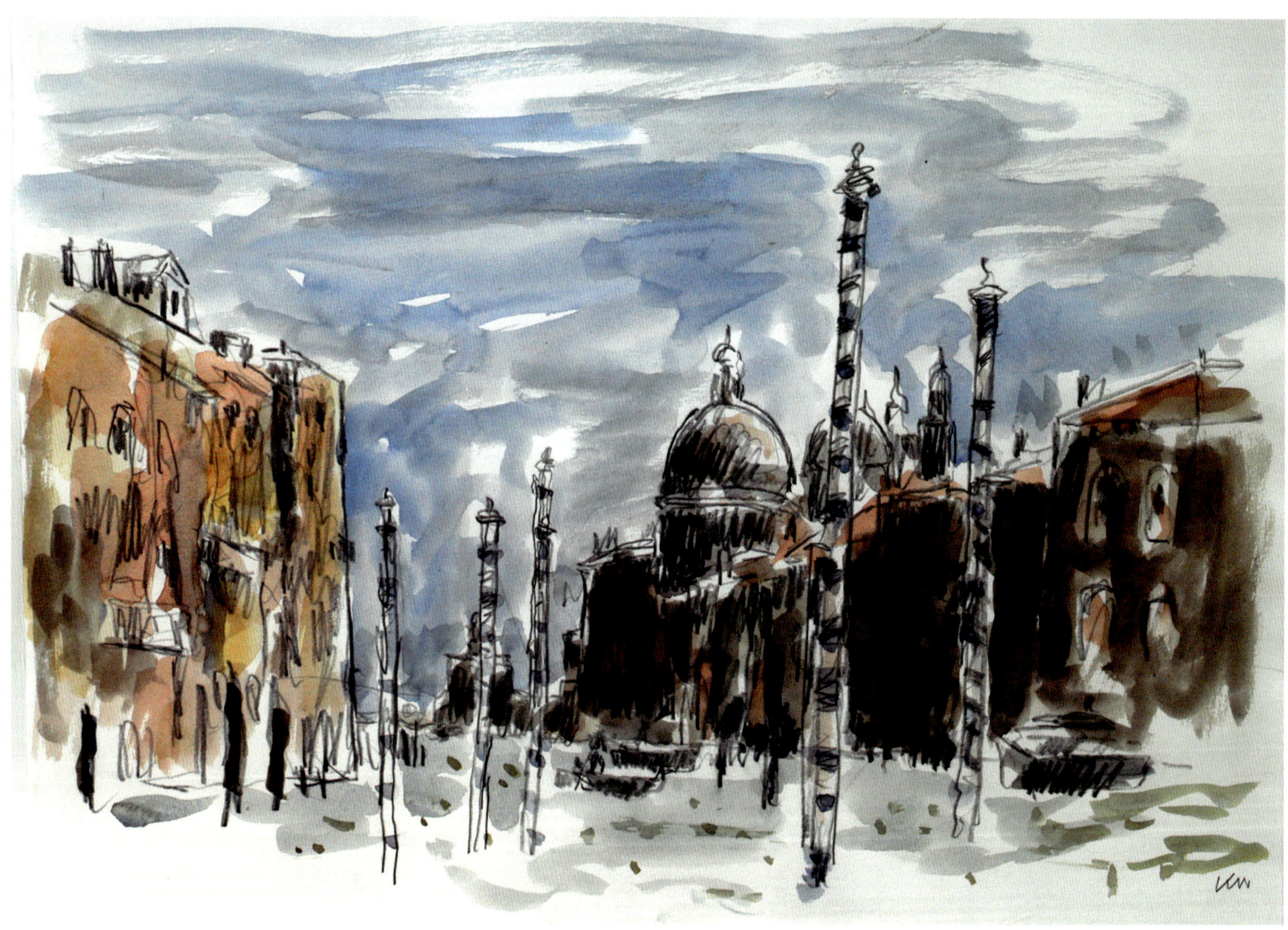

Santa Maria della Salute from Accademia Bridge, 2004

and singing but art somehow has always been on the sidelines and will remain on the sidelines until the Welsh people are able to see, in a gallery, the art of their own country. And they're not allowed to see it. This I find is absolutely tragic, because actually the Museum of Wales has wonderful paintings and sculptures by Welshmen. You go to the Museum of Wales and there are paintings by Richard Wilson. Even in Wales, people don't know him as a Welshman. The pictures are hanging but there's nothing to say he was a Welshman to make people proud of Richard Wilson, who had such an influence on English landscape paintings. And he was the link with Italian painting too.

Another is John Gibson of Conwy – he came from an Anglesey family. His father was a gardener in Anglesey, and the family was brought up in a house on an estate in Conwy, the Marl Estate. William Gibson, John Gibson's father, went over there to run the garden, about 1790, I think. John Gibson was apprenticed to a cabinetmaker in Liverpool, where he met sculptors, and then a man called Roscoe sent him to Rome to study under Canova and he became one of the three biggest neo-classical sculptors in the world – Canova, Thorwaldsen and John Gibson. He became immensely well known and he sculpted Sir Watkin Williams Wynn, who came out to Rome to see him, and another notable family, the Sandbachs of Hafodunos in Denbighshire – they commissioned him a lot – and he became a member of seven national academies including the Royal Academy. When he died, he was of such importance that the Emperor Napoleon, Louis Napoleon, sent a party of troops to Rome to

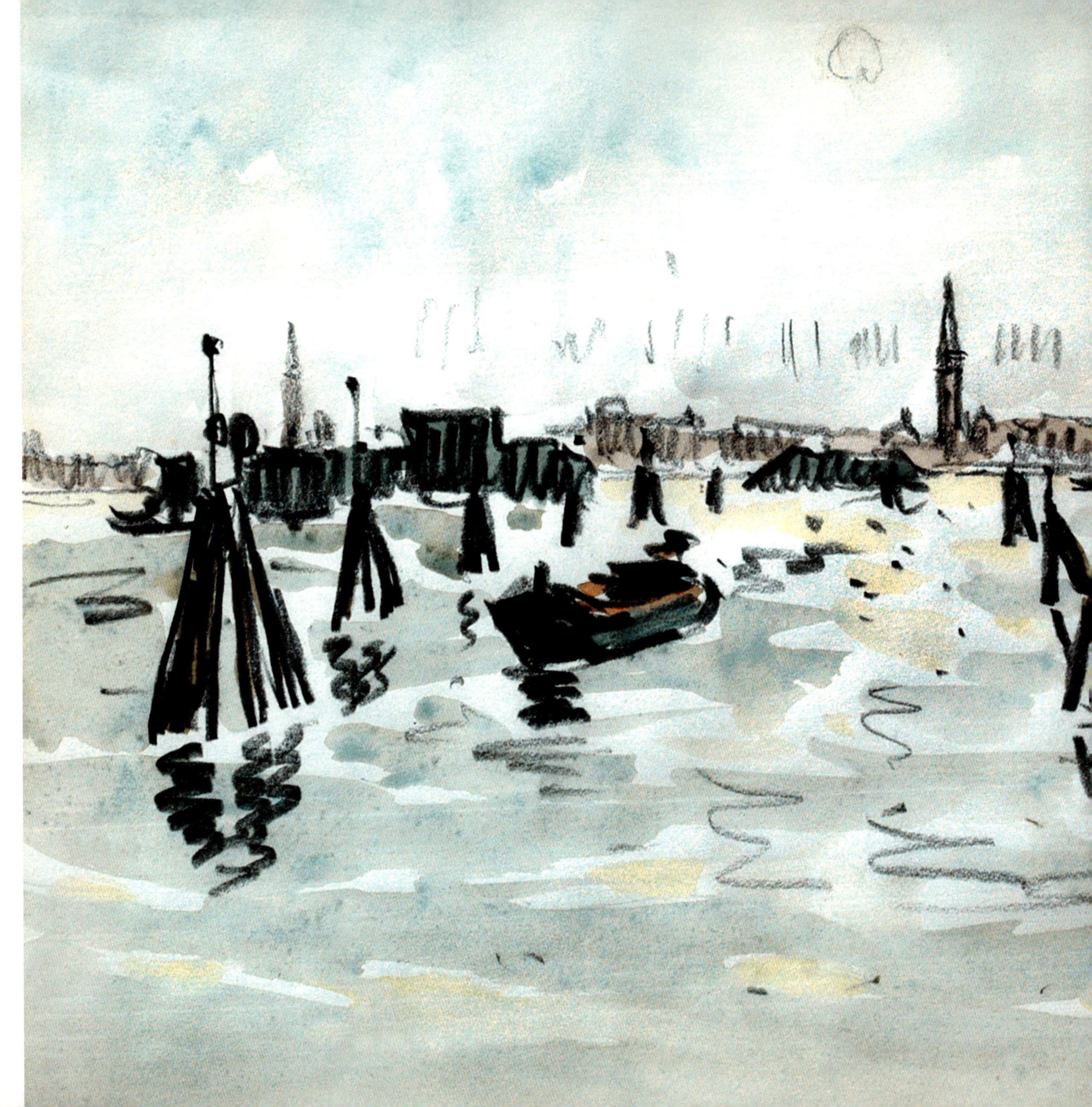

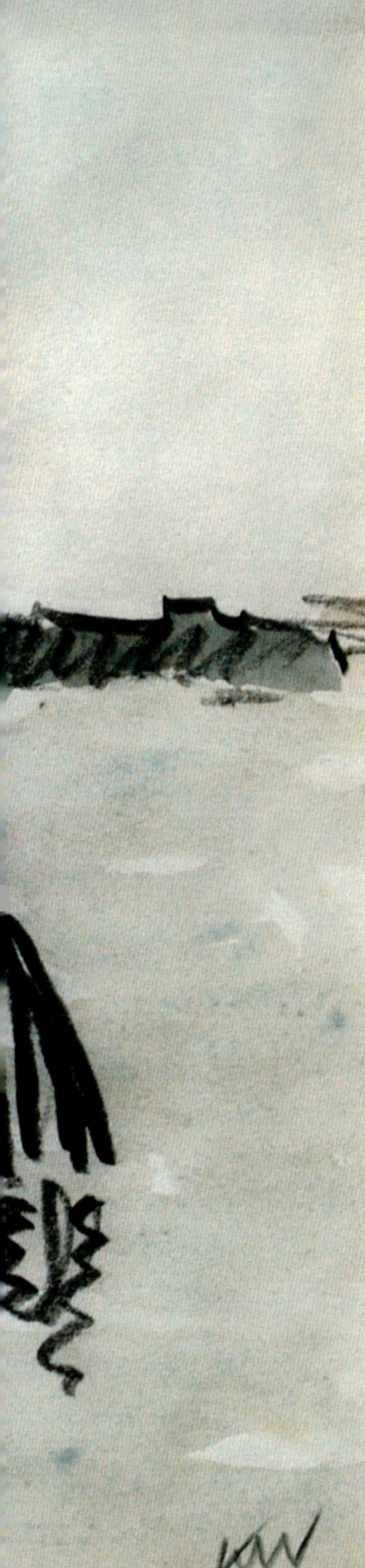

Barge in the Lagoon, 1979

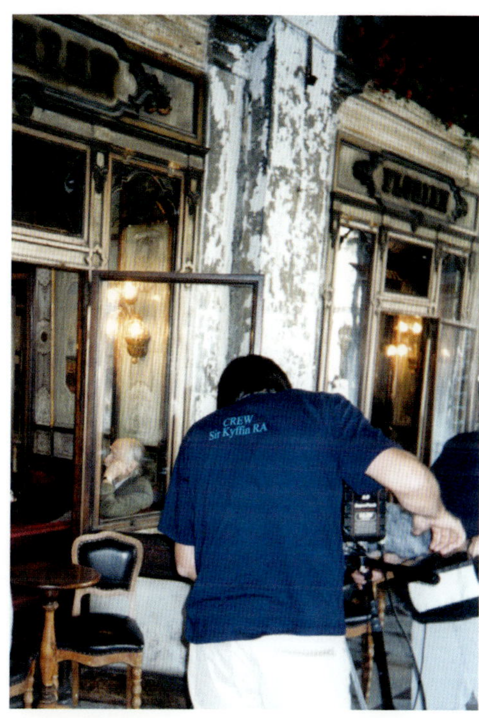

The camera crew at Caffè Florian

escort his body to the grave and to fire a volley over his grave. I mean he was that important, but in Wales nobody knows about him. You can buy postcards of his work in Rome railway station. The National Museum of Wales has recently bought two very fine Gibsons and they may have postcards of those but, otherwise, the man is pretty well unknown. I want Wales to appreciate the contribution made by artists in Wales. I want them really to be interested in art, visual art, the same way as they are interested in singing and poetry.

DM   Do you have faith that we will ever see such a development?

KW   I may not, but it will happen in the end, I'm sure. At the moment, art is in such a terrible state; it's at some sort of crossroads; there's a very conscious attempt by evil-minded people to destroy all tradition in art, because they believe that tradition is holding the future of art back. What these idiots do not understand is that art, or the tradition in art, is the outward expression of humanity and they're trying to kill humanity and there's no humanity in what is considered to be the new art of today now at all. I've always been absolutely aware of this.

DM   I was going to ask you what is your view of modern art and, linked with that, why is it that landscape painting these days is so much scorned, or perhaps I should say not appreciated?

KW   Well, the world of art has undoubtedly decided that it is of no importance in the future and you must realise that, in the whole history of art, which goes back 5000 years at least, the landscape has only taken up 600 years of that. The earliest pure landscapes were made before perspective was discovered but, as soon as perspective was discovered, the landscape could take off. The first real perspective was in the Low Countries in the Books of Hours by Pol de Limbourg and people like that: they're lovely little pictures of landscape, in very early perspective. This was quite a bit before perspective was done in Italy; people like Uccello, Piero della Francesca, they were the early people in there to discover perspective. Then Florence took off and Sienna held back; it didn't want to move on into that life. But another great part of the landscape came with the discovery of the oil medium and the place it really took off was Venice. They painted a lot in oil in the Low Countries and then Antonello moved up and wanted to go to Venice in 1474. He met a pupil of Van Eyck in Naples on the way – it might have been Petrus Christus, I don't know – but anyhow this pupil gave Antonello the secret of the oil medium. And when he got to Venice the next year, Giovanni Bellini, the most important artist of the time in Venice, got the secret of the oil medium from him. Luckily – one of the great bits of luck in the history of art – Venice at the time was a maritime power and in their shipyards there were acres of canvas and this oil medium was painted, more or less, as a substitute for the tempera painting in the Low Countries, whereas in Venice, suddenly, they had these acres of sailcloth and great artists like Titian, Tintoretto, Veronese, could paint huge pictures. The oil medium means you can use a brush more vigorously and fluently than if you're painting in tempera, for which you would use a small brush and the medium was the yolk of an egg – colour mixed with the yolk of an egg. So that was a tremendous thing for landscape painting – to paint the weather, clouds – that was a great moment in landscape painting.

Now unfortunately, our morning thinkers of today believe art must be of the future, and one of my greatest condemnations of what's called new art is the fact that there is no love in anything. Love is gone and they do not want any love to come back; they call it sentimental. No artist today will be recognised if he paints the head of a child. The head of a child is out. Sun shining over a valley or on the mountains, those are out. A student from Cardiff School of Art wrote to me once and said, 'We are told that landscape painting is a fascist art and a mindless love of nature which should not be done.' There's a thinking in the art world today that anything done with love, appreciation of something, is out. They've got to make statements of something which they can't create themselves; they have to get other people to paint them for them. People don't realise so much of modern art is totally incompetent technically. Maybe things are changing, I don't know, but a young student would be told to go into a room and express himself and then all the teachers would go off and have a glass of wine or coffee or something. That is how they were taught – Oh! go and express yourself. They were not taught at all. I sent a pupil from a school I taught at to the Royal

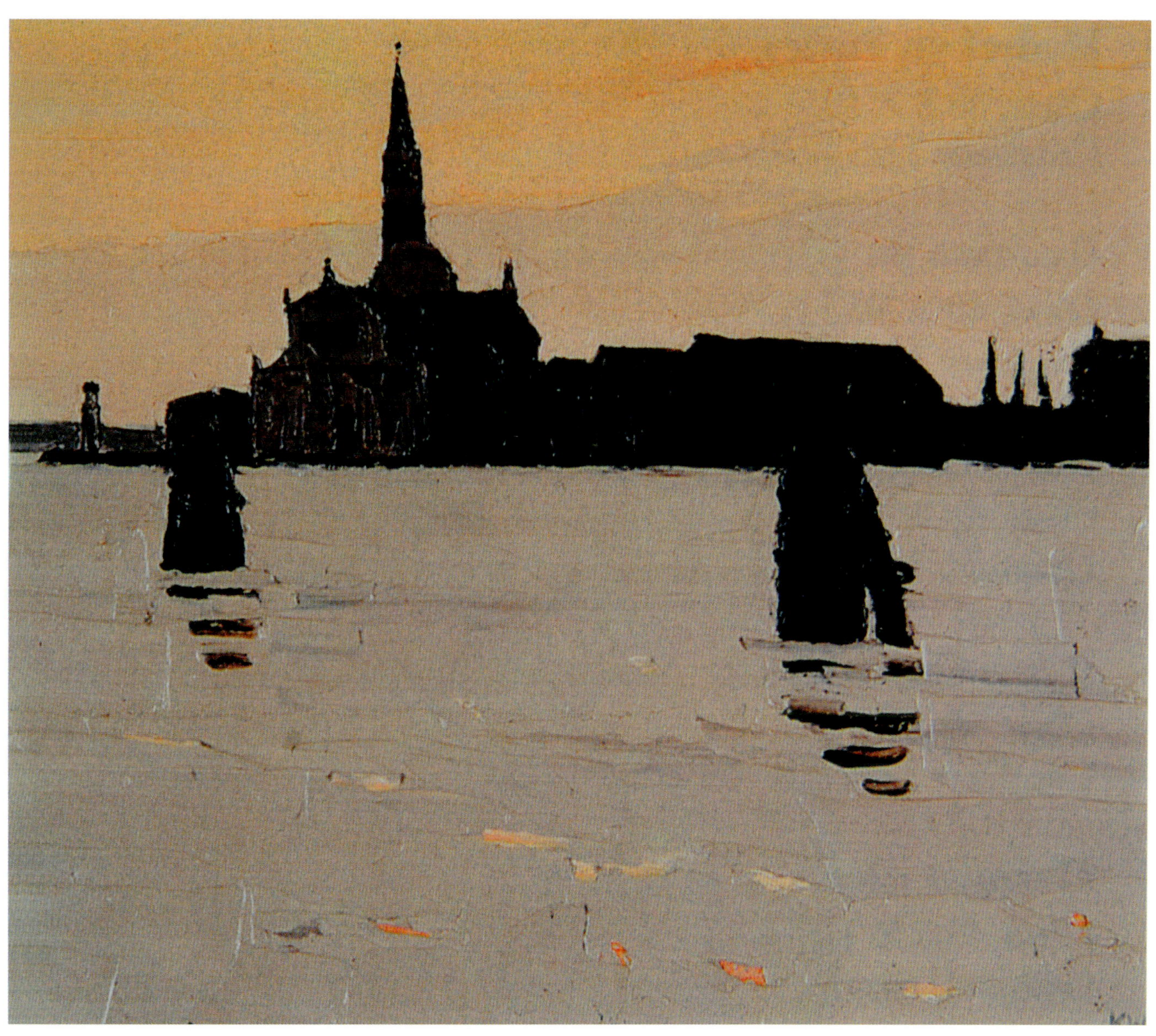

Sunrise, St Giorgio Maggiore, 1979

College; he was there four years. In four years, not one single teacher came to see his work, except after four years, one of the teachers came in through the door and said 'You've all got your ARCAs' and shut the door. That sort of teaching, it's all so ludicrous to me – 'thought' – because everybody thinks. The idea of going out, having a thought yourself, and getting other people to paint it for you. . . and yet there are pictures in galleries all over the world under a certain name but that artist has never touched the picture!

DM Do you see the proposed establishment of a modern art gallery in Wales as a step in the right direction?

KW I don't think this should happen. There's no such thing as modern art. That's what makes it all so stupid. I mean from the beginning of time, and until the end of time, there's only good, bad and indifferent art. Do what they like and say what they like, that is true of most modern artists, and some are really bad. This is the great 'modern art' which is supposed to be taking the place of traditional art. But you cannot destroy tradition. Tradition is in the soul of the people. Amen.

DM You're venerated by society, honoured with a knighthood, your paintings hang in our national centres – I'm thinking of the National Assembly for Wales these days, for example

– and yet, from time to time, the National Museum of Wales has appeared indifferent to your advice regarding purchasing works of art, for instance, and the Arts Council has appeared to me to have been a hindrance on occasion. Why has this been?

KW   When you consider the National Museum, it's the National Museum of Wales, and as such, they can do two things, one or the other, to be successful. One is they want it to be a museum which is on the same level as the great museums of Europe – the Prado in Madrid, the Louvre in Paris, the Albertina in Vienna, the Rijks museum in Amsterdam, for example – but the problem is they can all afford it; they have a wonderful collection going back to the year dot. Here in Wales, they'd like the National Museum to be on that level, and so I sometimes feel that in order to try to be on that level, they ignore the art of Wales. But it's a difficult position for them and I disagree with them quite a lot over various things, but there we are, they've got to look at it in that way.

DM   I believe you had a problem with Gwen John, for instance, when you suggested the Museum should buy one of her paintings?

KW   Yes, well they didn't really care for Gwen John; that was very interesting. I got a wonderful letter from them saying that she was of little worth. I didn't keep that letter, unfortunately!

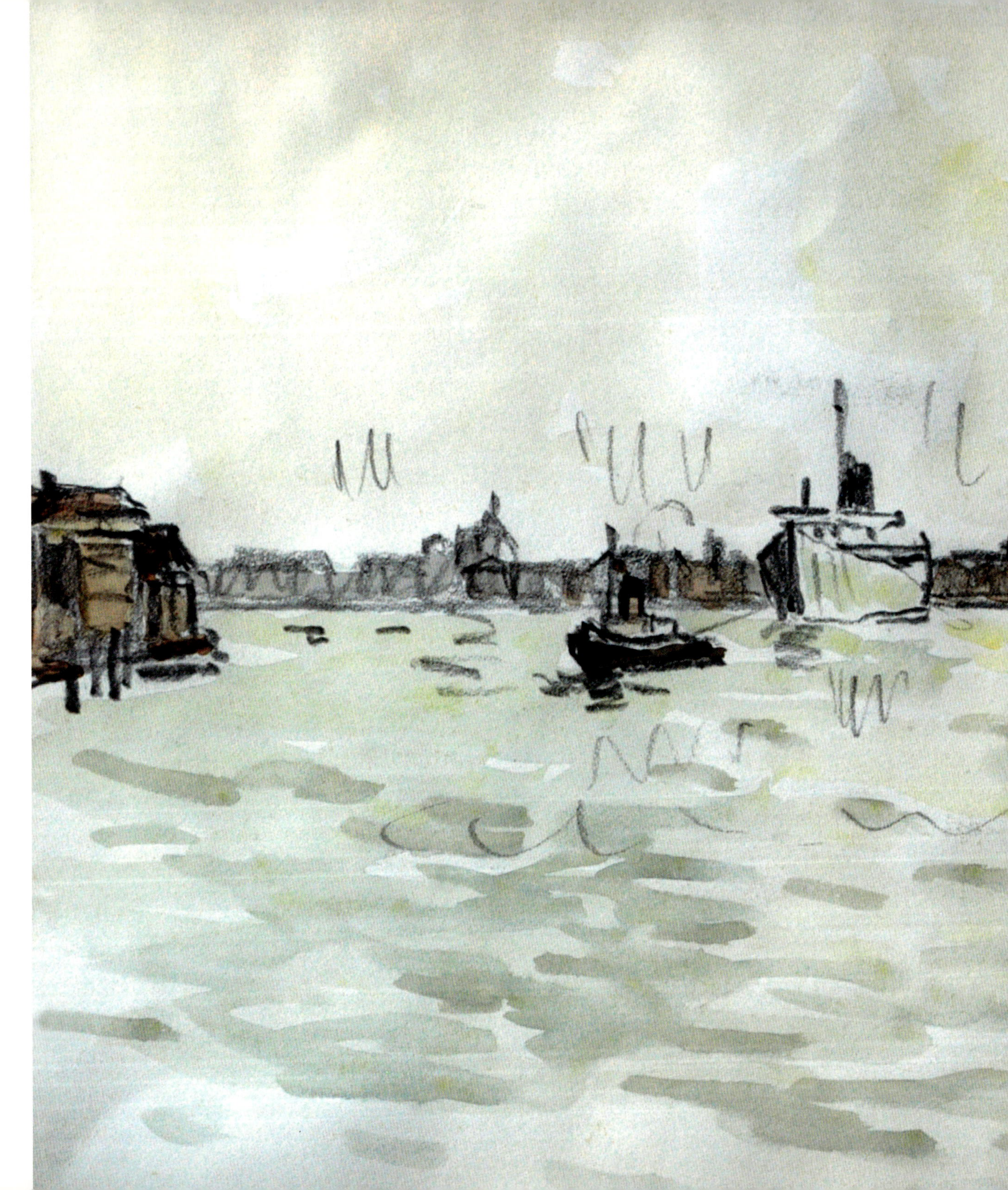

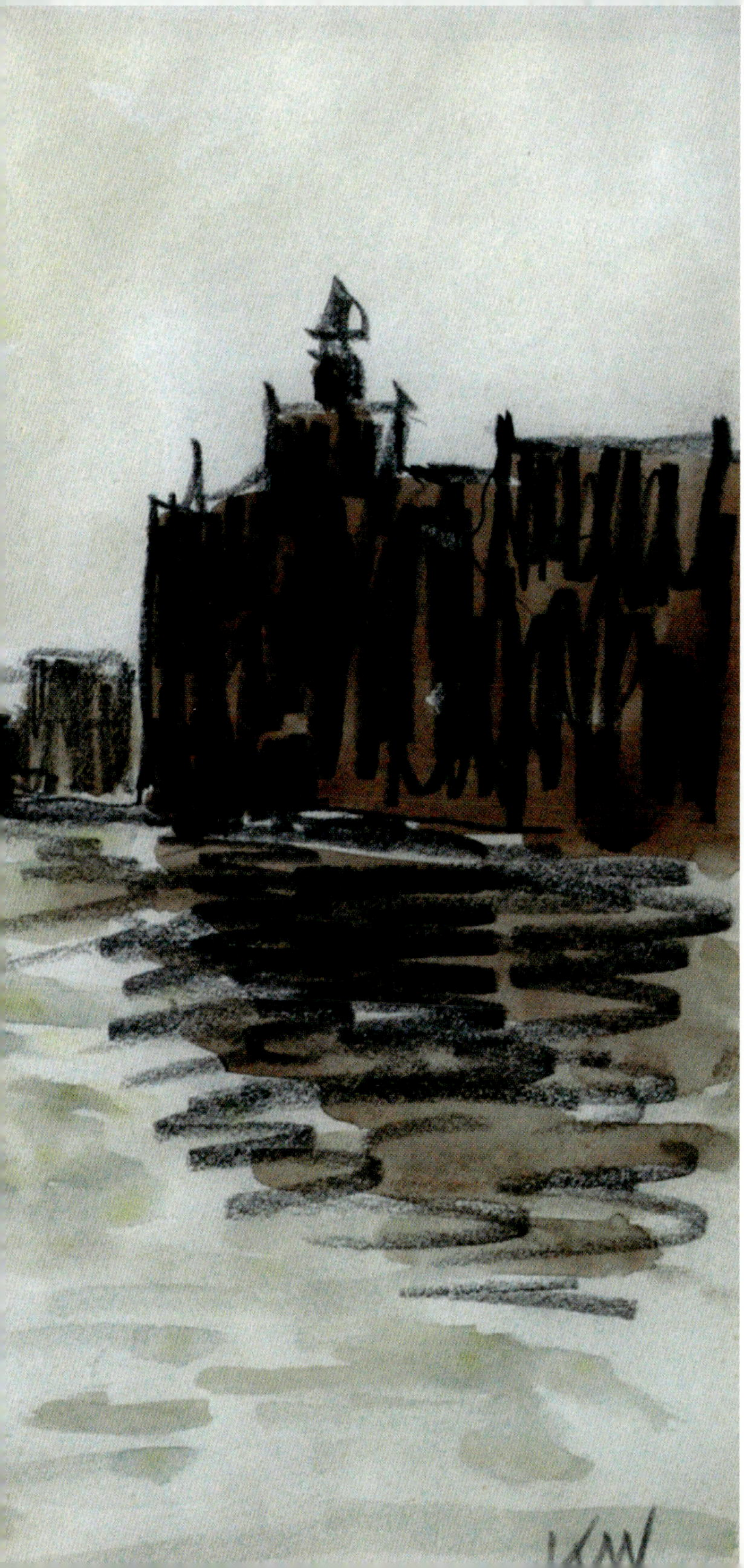

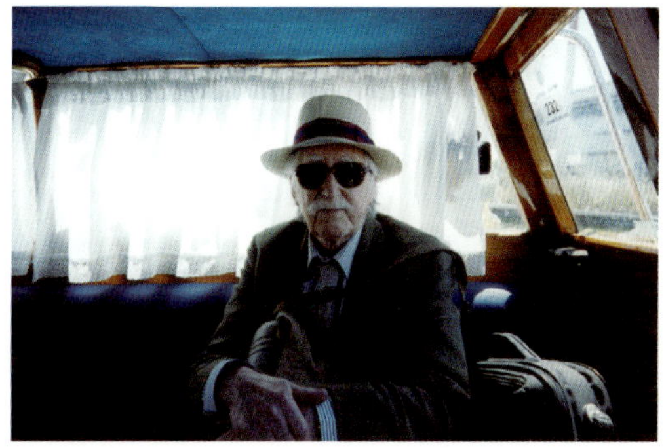

In the water taxi

Liner off the Giudecca, 1979

But, I got on with the keepers even though I disagreed with them very much. I remember I asked one keeper, quite some time ago, if, when he was purchasing a work of art, he considered whether it would be liked by the Welsh public. And he said, 'Well, if ever I considered the opinions of the Welsh public, I know that would be the time for me to give up my job.' And that, I think, is rather odd. I'm always very keen on getting as much Welsh art of merit as possible in Wales' National Gallery, but that job seems to have been taken up by the National Library. They buy a tremendous number of work by Welsh artists, and the real record is there – not the very best Welsh pictures by Richard Wilson maybe, but certainly since the War, they've taken over more or less the job of the National Museum. The National Museum buys works by Ceri Richards, Josef Herman and people like that, but the John Elwyns of this world are mainly bought by the National Library.

DM   And there's an excellent collection there by now.

KW   That's right. A very, very good collection of Welsh art; they have a bit of everybody really, and they continue to buy works by Welsh artists. You see with portraits, the National Portrait Gallery of Wales is split between the National Museum and the Library. The National Museum buys portraits of Welsh artists if those portraits are a work of art. If they're not a work of art but a record, they go to the National Library. In that way, quite a number of pictures have come to the National Library which are works or art as well as being records, but they do have quite a good collection.

DM   I well remember you and I going to visit Kate Roberts, that great literary figure, and I think the portrait that you drew of her that day is a marvellous portrait.

KW   That was terribly difficult. She'd had strokes and things. She was almost immobile. She could hardly speak and she sat hugely in a big chair rather like the hulk of a once-proud battleship. She sat there and looked at me. I knew that her brain was perfectly all right and I knew that if I did a drawing of what was in front of me, she wouldn't like it at all, so it had to be an expressionist drawing and a terrifying drawing. Really, she did look terrifying. So I had to be hypocritical and devious and I did a drawing of a distinguished-looking old lady and then after I finished, she looked at me and she waggled her finger – she wanted to have a look at it you see. So, with great trepidation, I took it along to her, a little smile at the corner of her mouth and she just said *'Da iawn'* – very good – that's all. I went home then and being the devious man that I am, I used that as a springboard to do my final drawing, but I didn't have the heart to make a really expressionist drawing of how she was – she looked terrifying. So I did a sort of an in-between. And that portrait now is in the National Library in Aberystwyth

DM You painted Alun Oldfield Davies, the former Controller at BBC Wales. He was a tall man and you painted him full length. Why did you choose to do that?

KW I was commissioned to paint him for the BBC, and he came and sat for me. He was about 6'5" or 6'6"; he was enormous and he sat in the chair and he crossed his gigantic legs and I painted him sort of behind his legs and shoes. He had a face which resembled a spider's web – lines went out from the centre and it was mainly lines in his face – but he was very good humoured and a very gentle, kind man, I thought. Anyhow I painted his portrait and the BBC wanted to see it before they paid for it. So I had it photographed and sent them a photograph. I got a letter back saying 'We consider this picture to be repellent'. The word 'repellent' struck me to be rather fierce and I didn't really like being called a repellent painter and so I said, well, look here, you'd better get somebody like Tom Rathmell to paint him because he could handle it – I didn't say because of all the lines on the face – but anyhow, Alun Oldfield refused to be painted by anyone but me. So in order to put him off, I said, 'Well, next time you'll have to stand for your portrait.' And he said, 'That's fine by me.' When he came, he stood in the corner of my studio, rather like an Atlas missile, and I painted him in all full length and full size. It took me only a day to do this. The thing was, I had to give the effect of height. You have to use a trick for this: in order to make someone look tall, you have to cut their feet off in the painting, because then you never know how long the legs will go on until you get to the feet! So if you've a very tall man, that's what you do, and that's what I did! I have made him look immensely tall and they accepted this painting.

DM   Kyffin, somebody once said that success in Wales today means having a house in Pontcanna in Cardiff, a Volvo in the garage and a Kyffin on the wall. How do you feel being this status symbol?

KW   I've got a Volvo myself. I'm very happy to be involved in Volvos. I don't know about Pontcanna, but my family came from a parish called Llansadwrn and Saint Sadwrn was married to a Canna.

DM   And in Pontcanna you've got street names like Cyfeiliog Street, Teilo Street, so a very saintly area, as well as being fashionable! But are the visual arts fashionable today in Wales?

KW   It concerns me greatly that the Welsh public are not really geared to visual arts and I do dearly want to try and awaken the people of Wales to the visual arts, because there's so much passion in Wales which could let loose if only they could be made to be interested. And at the National Eisteddfod of Wales, fine art takes a minor part now they've gone all for

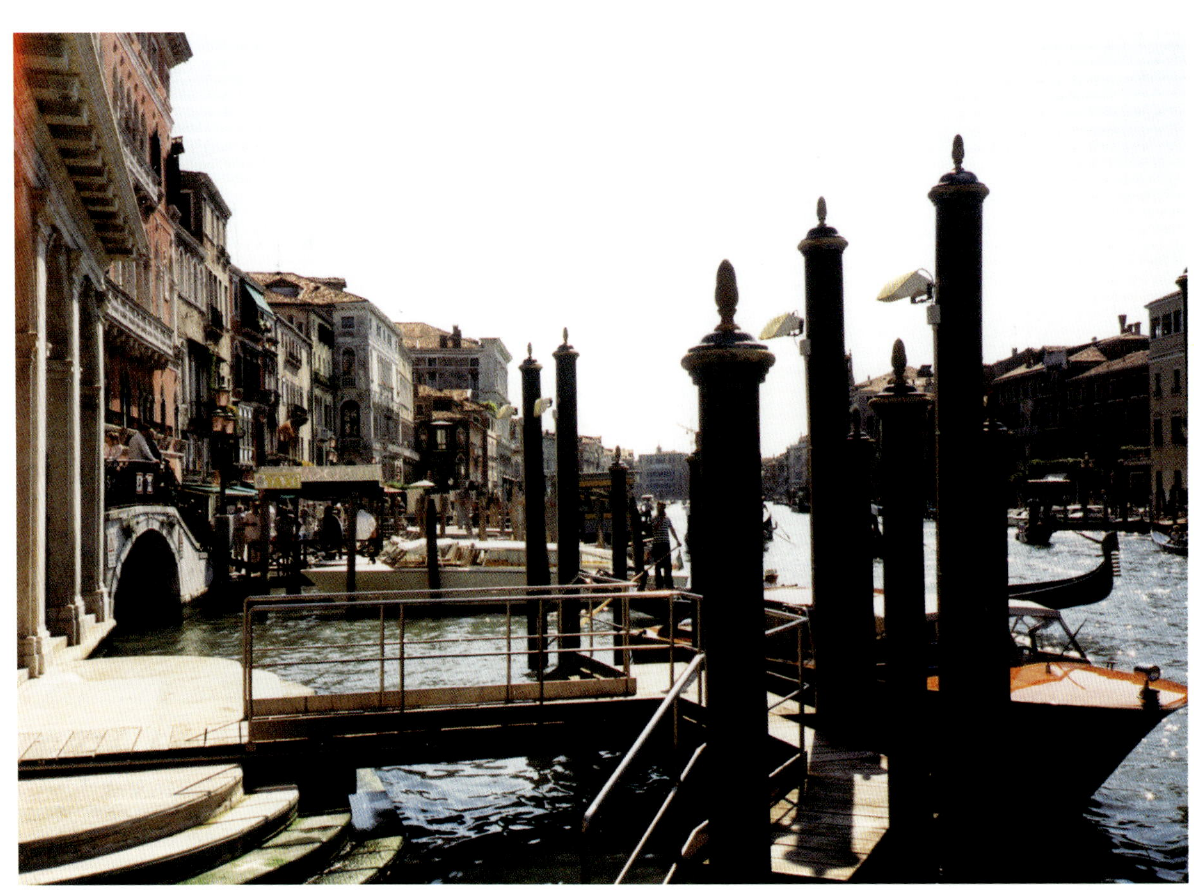

62   Mooring posts, Grand Canal

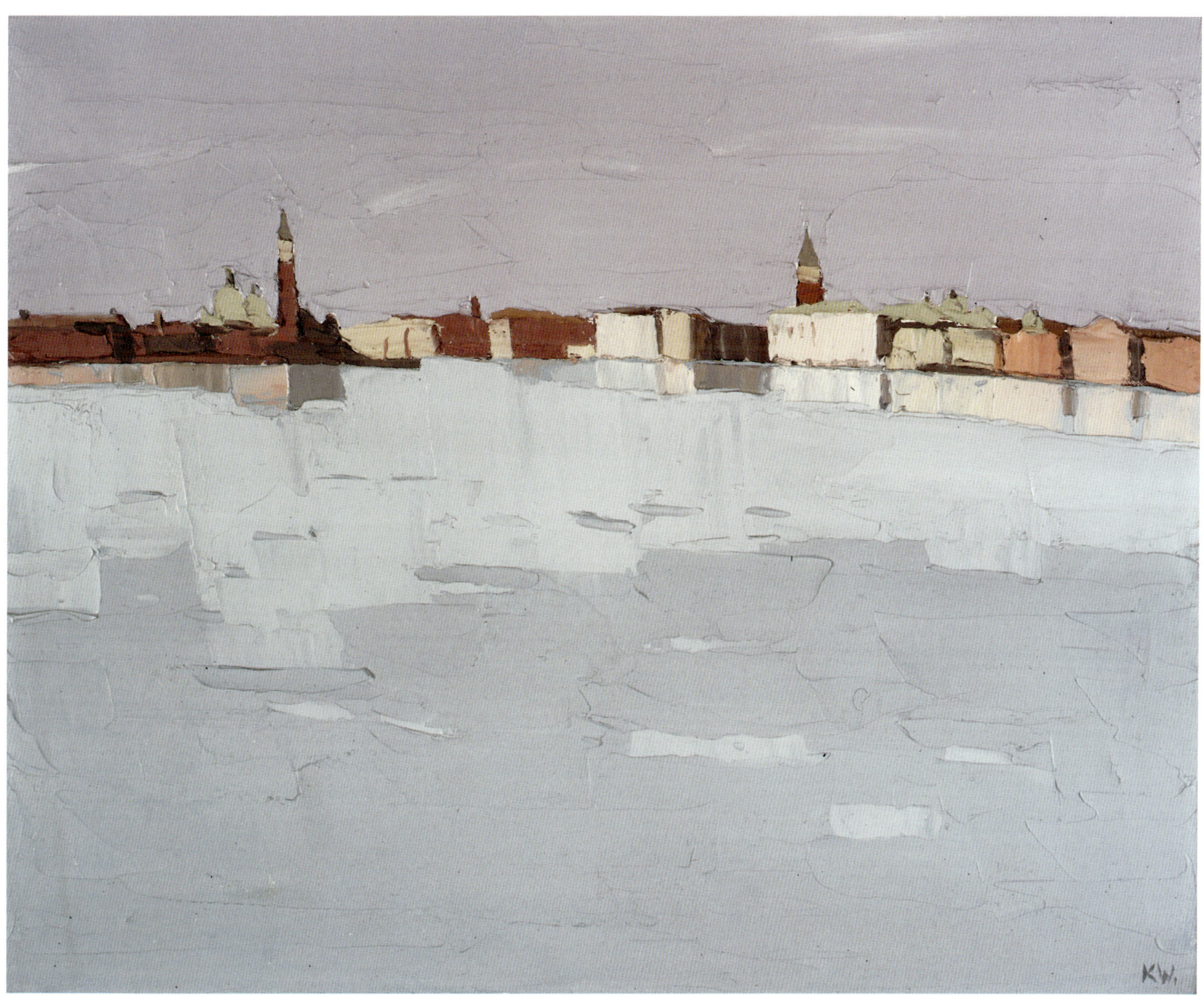

Venice from the Gardens, 1979

avant garde and they show the most ridiculous things. This drives the public away. People don't actually go to the Arts and Crafts because they get so offended by what they're shown. This I think should be changed.

DM Thinking of art in Wales today, and thinking in particular of Peter Lord, the author and art historian, how do you rank his contribution?

KW Well I've got great admiration for Peter Lord. He was wonderfully obsessive. I knew he was an obsessive painter, but he was wonderfully obsessive about art and he really wanted to show that Wales was not the backroad artistic country that most people think of us. He tried to find as much about Welsh painters as possible and resurrect their reputation and he became absolutely dedicated to this. He worked immensely hard going round Wales, finding out about all these artists; Hugh Hughes was one of his heroes; he was a Llandudno man I think. Lord was dedicated to writing about things in Wales and he showed us all the artists who came to Betws y Coed in the time of David Cox and Clarence Waite and maybe it's a good thing that he was an Englishman dedicated to Wales and that all these artists, Cox and Clarence Waite, were Englishmen who were also dedicated to Wales, because Lord showed the people of Wales what had been going on and we have to thank him very much for this scholarship. He really was a scholar who did a tremendous amount for Wales and I hope that he will go on doing a lot for Wales. He's a very outspoken man but the only way you can get anything done, really, is by being outspoken.

DM   And jumping from Peter Lord to Graham Sutherland, he has painted a lot in Wales, as you know so well. Do you regard his paintings as Welsh?

KW   Well I think Graham Sutherland is a very fine artist. He's been very badly treated by the world of art. I don't like the world of art; it's insensitive and arrogant. They praised Sutherland in his lifetime as being the greatest landscape painter since Turner, and they went on praising him like mad until he died and then they hit him – he was no good, he was a poor artist and everything; all the critics dumped him. I thought that to be monstrous. They have to find something to write about so they decide to kill off Graham Sutherland. But he was a nice man, Graham Sutherland, and he was a very good artist. I think I probably liked him best as a graphic artist – he wasn't a painter. Two artists who are very well-known, good artists, John Piper and Sutherland, they weren't painters. They didn't handle paint well. They used it to stain the canvas really. Sutherland is best known, in a way, for his Pembrokeshire paintings but I do not share the enthusiasm of the art world for these paintings. You see, I believe that Sutherland wanted to paint Pembrokeshire when he was in London, and in London he thought up how he would interpret Pembrokeshire without having been there. When he first went down to Pembrokeshire, he went with closed eyes and he couldn't really see the true Pembrokeshire in front of him; so he'd been on the roots of the trees on the Cleddau River and there were oranges and lime greens and colours of citrus and melons, which you'd never see there, and he produced all these colours, produced a Pembrokeshire the likes of which the people of Pembrokeshire had never seen before. They were good pictures, there's no doubt about it, they were good pictures but they were not in my mind an interpretation of the landscape. Artists very often get the wrong end of the stick. I once met a good artist called John Craxton – he's now a member of the Royal Academy – and he said he'd been down to Pembrokeshire with Graham and he'd seen how remarkable the peasants were in Pembrokeshire! I never think of Welsh people as peasants! He said that they're remarkable people, how they raise up phallic symbols in their fields in order to inspire fertility in their flocks. Well, I thought immediately of the old scratching stone. But then he said they painted fertility murals on the roofs of their houses! That really pushed me – I'd never seen a fertility mural on a roof of a house. Then I went back to Pembrokeshire, and I saw how, because of the wind, the slate roofs were grouted to keep the slates on and then the grouting cracks were filled in with different coloured paint so there are lines and circles and things. So these must have been interpreted by somebody from England as fertility murals, and that I think maybe Graham Sutherland thought in the same way; he interpreted it in an intellectual way and not in an emotional way.

DM Kyffin, to me your Venice paintings are inspirational. What brought you to Venice in the first place?

KW I never thought of them being inspirational. What amazed me about Venice is that I got the distinct impression it was a very colourful place, but it's not colourful. If you go up into the Alps it gets colourful because of the air; down at sea level it becomes subtle and, to me, it is best when the sky gets very dark blue-black and all the palazzos along the Grand Canal become silvery, rather like in the work of Guardi. His paintings, more than Canaletto's, I think, got the feeling of Venice . . .

DM More than Canaletto?

KW Well, Canaletto is a greater painter, without a doubt, but in the interpretation of Venice, in a way I feel I prefer Guardi. But anyhow, Venice really had a great influence on the development of landscape painting. Of course Rubens was in Venice and he used to see the landscape background of the paintings of Titian. Rubens in his old age painted the Chateau de Steen, which was a wonderful painting, and then of course that was bought by a man called Harvey in Norwich and taken over to Norwich. I think, without any shadow of a doubt, Constable must have seen it and his painting of 'The Hay Wain' comes

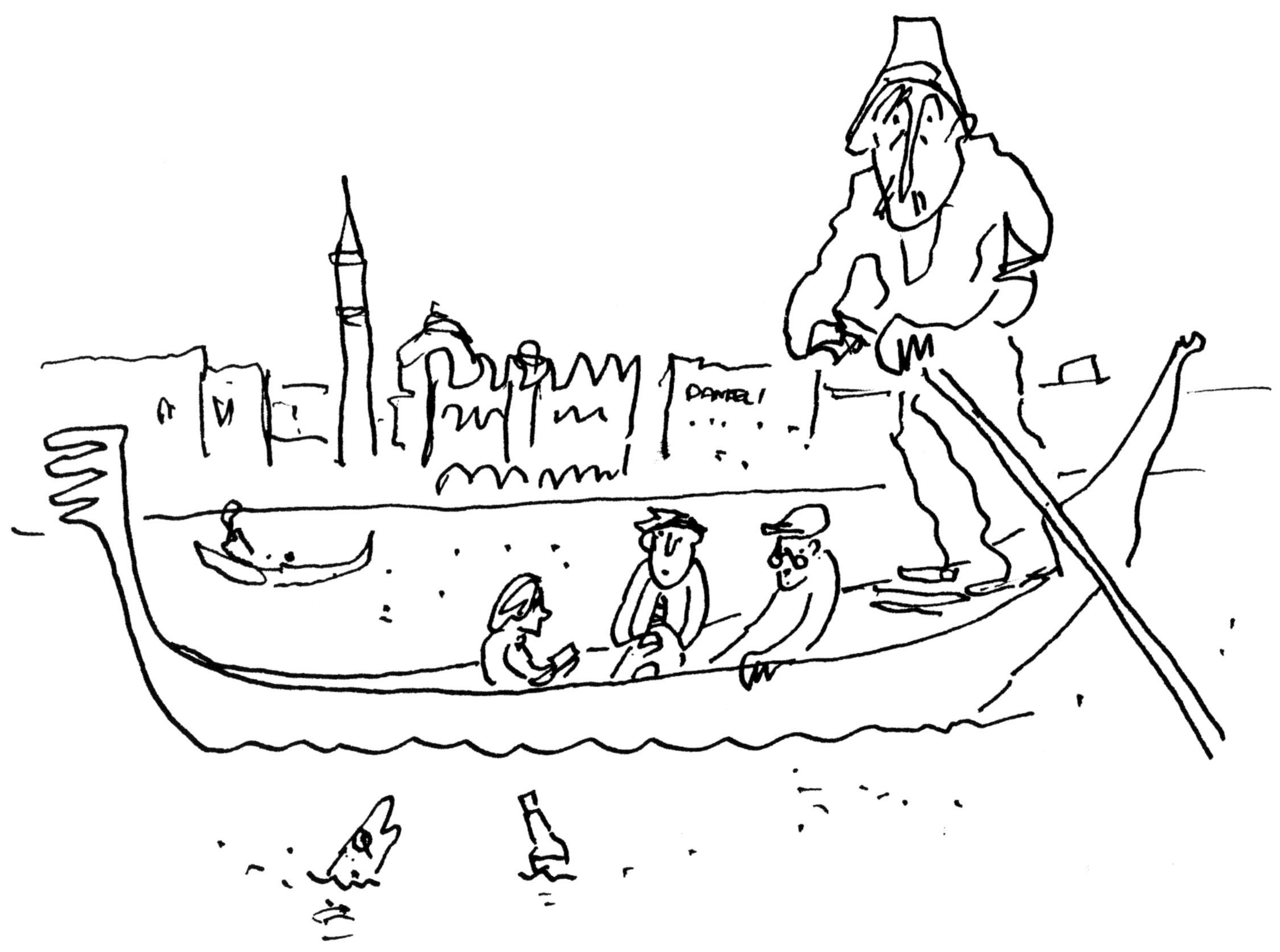

 Kyffin, gondola with tourists (a thank you note to John Hefin)

directly from the Chateau de Steen. And then, it was a great influence in the development of landscape painting, even in people like Delacroix, and that is the importance of Venice in landscape painting and the romantic development within art.

DM Kyffin, you've changed your style of painting over the years, especially I'm thinking of your style of painting the mountains. What brought about that change?

KW Oh, I don't think I have changed, really. But I found I could produce the effect of light. I love the light hitting – when it comes through the clouds and the clouds are moving – and the light hits on the breast of a hill and shines against the rather flatness of the darkness in the hills, and I've evolved a way of painting with a palette knife in which I mix about three colours, or maybe four, but I don't completely mix them, so I've got a strand of white, a strand of black, a strand of yellow ochre and maybe a strand of cobalt green, and you lay it on and because the colours aren't actually mixed up, each colour shows slightly in the paint and it gives a shimmer. This happened first when I was painting a portrait, painting the light on a girl's cheek; I used it there and after this I found to my horror that I was beginning to use this trick consciously: I realised I was using my paint for the sake of the paint rather than the subject, and that is totally wrong in my way of thinking. I mean, with abstract painting there is no question of the subject, but the subject was always more important to me than the old tricks of painting. The new type of painting started way back at the end of the nineteenth century with the Fauve movement, that the object they are painting is more important than the subject. That, I believe, is the beginning of modern art, where the object is more important than the subject. It means they're slightly divorced away from the love of the thing. I love Fauve paintings but that was the beginning of it. They'd seen the work of Van Gogh and the wonderful colour and one forgot that the colour was inspired by the subject. Now they used the colour for colour's sake. They'd probably say 'Oh if I had that sky purple, well, these hills would be a lovely orangey colour'. It's totally different, all about being clever, not being loving, not being moved by the landscape or people or something like that.

DM   You've recently been painting flowers in oil, the flowers that grow around your home at Pwllfanogl. Is this a recent departure?

KW   I've always painted flowers; I've always liked flowers but people don't realise I do paint flowers. It's a wonderful way for trying to do something with colour. Maybe colour is not one of my strong points.

DM   I beg to disagree.

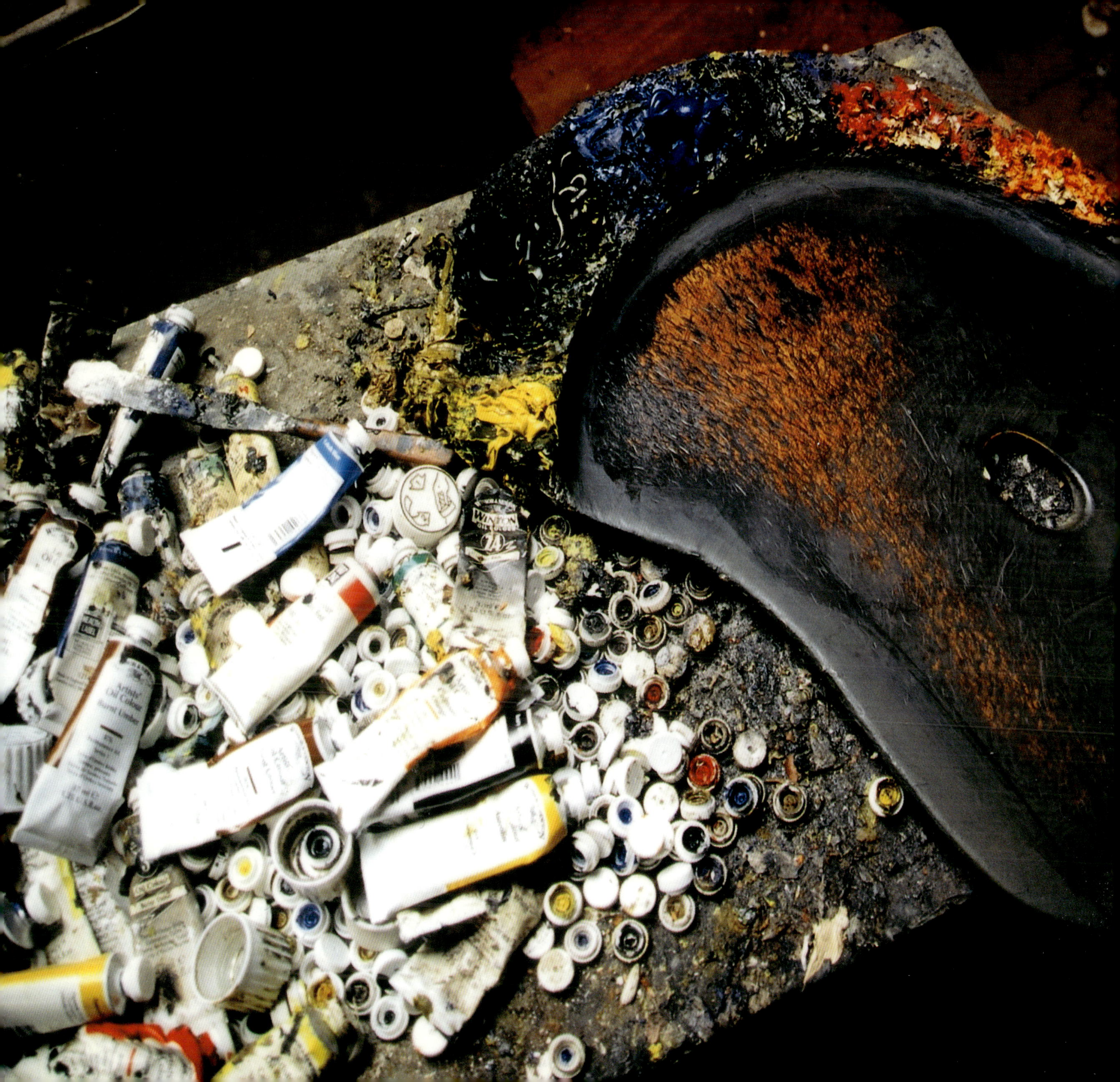

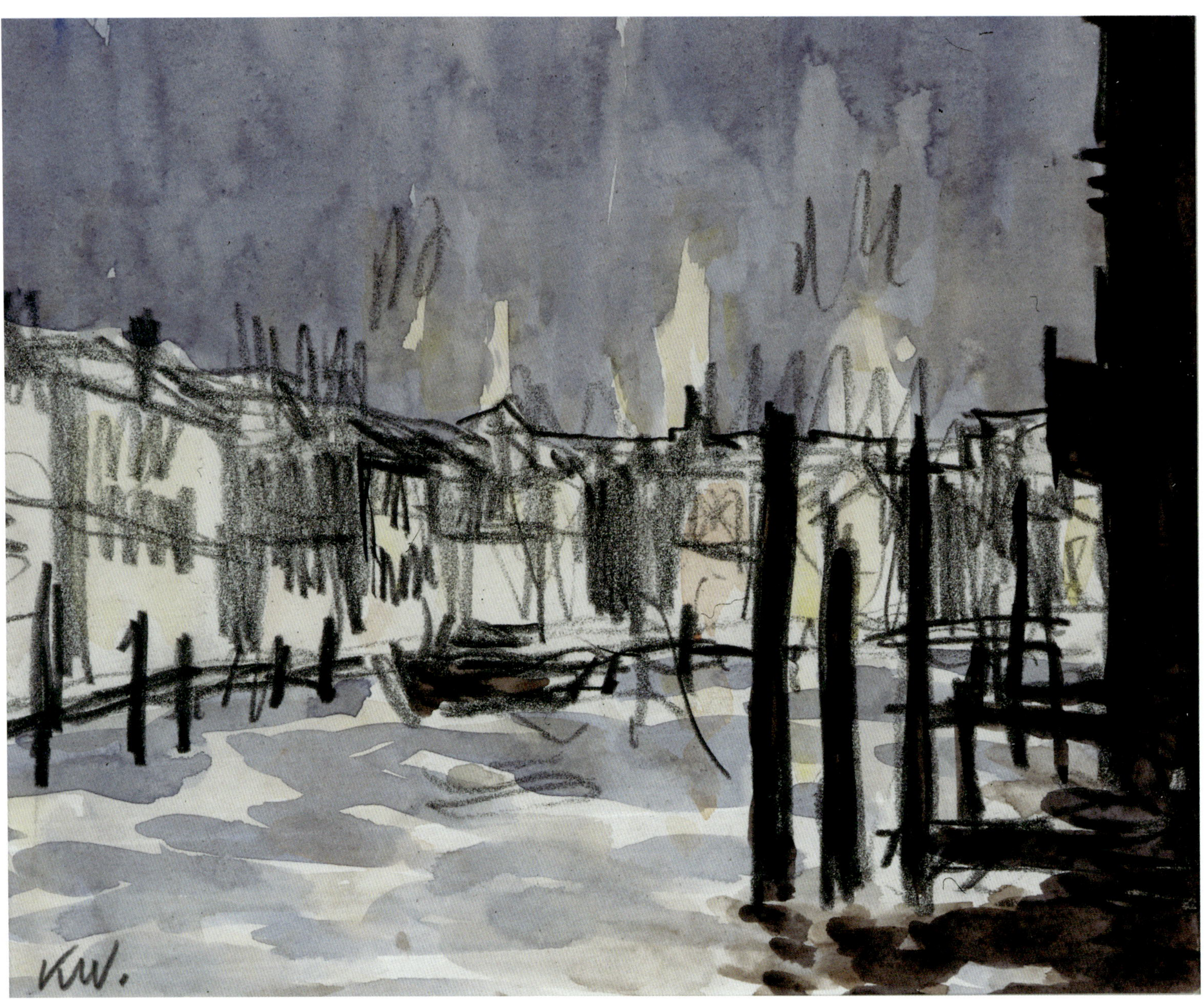

KW   I'm not a colourist. A colourist is somebody like Matisse, who is a juggler. He can throw up ten colours in the air and catch them all, whereas I can only throw up four balls of colour and catch them. If I tried five, I'd fall flat on my face. No, it's something slightly different. Anyhow, I love flowers, I love the freshness of flowers but I don't do nearly as much as I should.

DM   I heard once that you had to pay for a humanitarian act with a painting; is it true that you had difficulty with your car on one occasion?

KW   Oh lord yes. Well, I was drawing on Traeth Coch in Anglesey, on the shoreline, and I wanted to drive across the sand. I started off and after a bit the car started to sink and I started to panic. I stopped people to get me out; they couldn't. Eventually I went to a farmer nearby and he was wonderful, he was very imperious – 'Right, Mr Williams is stuck in the sand, come on, get him out,' – and he got them all down and he got them all round my car and then he said, 'When I say lift, you lift.' They all got round my car, there was a sucking sound and my car came out. I was terribly grateful but I didn't know what to do: he wasn't the sort of man you could tip. So I gave him a drawing which I'd just been doing and he looked at it, 'Oh, oh yes,' he said, and he folded it into four and put it in his pocket. So I went back to do another drawing and that actually turned out to be a better drawing, thank goodness.

DM   He probably thought it was a map!

KW   Another time on Traeth Coch I remember, I wanted to go across the shore and there was a farm labourer who I didn't know, so I went out and asked him, 'How do you get across to the other side?' And he said, 'Well you see that tree up there, get that in line with that big stone there, and go straight.' So I did that. I went absolutely straight and again, my car started to sink. I didn't know what to do. Suddenly I saw him coming across very slowly over the sand. When he got up to me, he pulled out a huge pocket watch and he said, 'Well, you will have to be pretty slippy; the tide is up in twenty minutes!'

DM   We've already discussed the fact that you portray people and places, would you agree that people in the end are more important than places?

KW   I do believe that people are more important than places. A lot of places are important because people live in places and *cynefin* is something which is very important, I think, and the love of an area. People have always been important in my family. I come from a long line of parsons on every possible side of my family and my ancestors were parsons. Of course they were all acutely tied up with the people. I was brought up on stories of all these people – Jack One Eye, Wil 'Refail and all these characters. My father would tell stories about Lisa

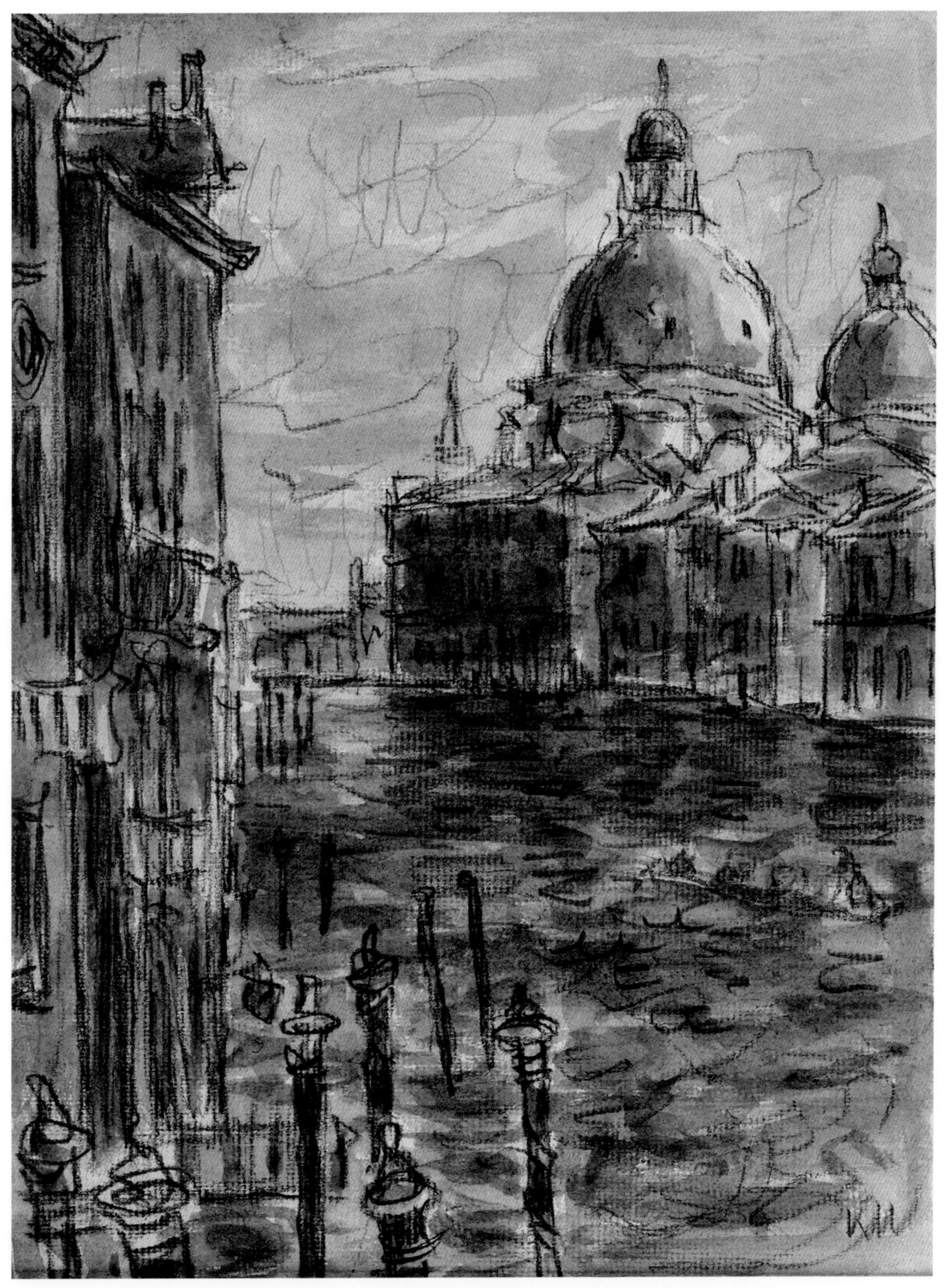

Matharn-Isaf and all these characters, and I was brought up to appreciate these people. When my grandfather was appointed to a living at Llanrhuddlad, right on the north-west corner of Anglesey, where my great-grandfather was and my great-great-grandfather, there were always people there when we used to go to stay there with my father. You see, it's a long way from the social life of Anglesey, which was in those days Beaumaris. It's about a day's riding by horse to get there so he didn't go there very often. So all his friends were the cottagers and the farm boys and when we went to stay there, we'd have to go out to all the farms and they became terribly important, these people. That's why I really love painting the people, the farm people, and that sort of thing more than anybody else.

DM   You mention sculpture a great deal, and sculptors. Are there any sculptors that really stand out?

KW   Oh, there's a tremendous number of them. I love these magnificent equestrian statues. There's one in Venice, the Colleone statue. It's a magnificent thing, this arrogant man. Funnily enough, when I went to Patagonia, I found that the Gauchos and the Welsh there rode with the same arrogance as the Colleone statue. They rode with one shoulder forward, looking magnificently like knights. Anyhow, another excellent one is Condottiere Gatamalata in Padua, and then there's Marcus Aurelius in Rome.

DM   And in Wales?

KW Well, I can think of Ivor Roberts Jones's statute, 'Horse and Man', based on Bendigeidfran coming back from the wars in Ireland. Unfortunately for poor old Bendigeidfran, only his head came back.

DM   You had a central role in Ivor Roberts Jones's sculpture of Churchill, at Westminster?

KW   Well, Ivor was a very good friend of mine and he was commissioned to do the statute of Churchill. He had a terrible time getting the commission because Lady Churchill didn't want a Welshman to do it. A terrible battle. I sought the help of Lord Cledwyn over this and he was wonderful; he helped a lot . . .

DM   The arch diplomat . . .

KW   Yes. In the end, it got going and I was told to get on with the work on condition it might never be put up, because old Clemmie was being very difficult about it. Anyhow, I went over to see the statue in Ivor's studio while he was doing it and he'd got the coat all wrong. He hadn't had anybody to pose for him so he hadn't got the greatcoat right. So I said

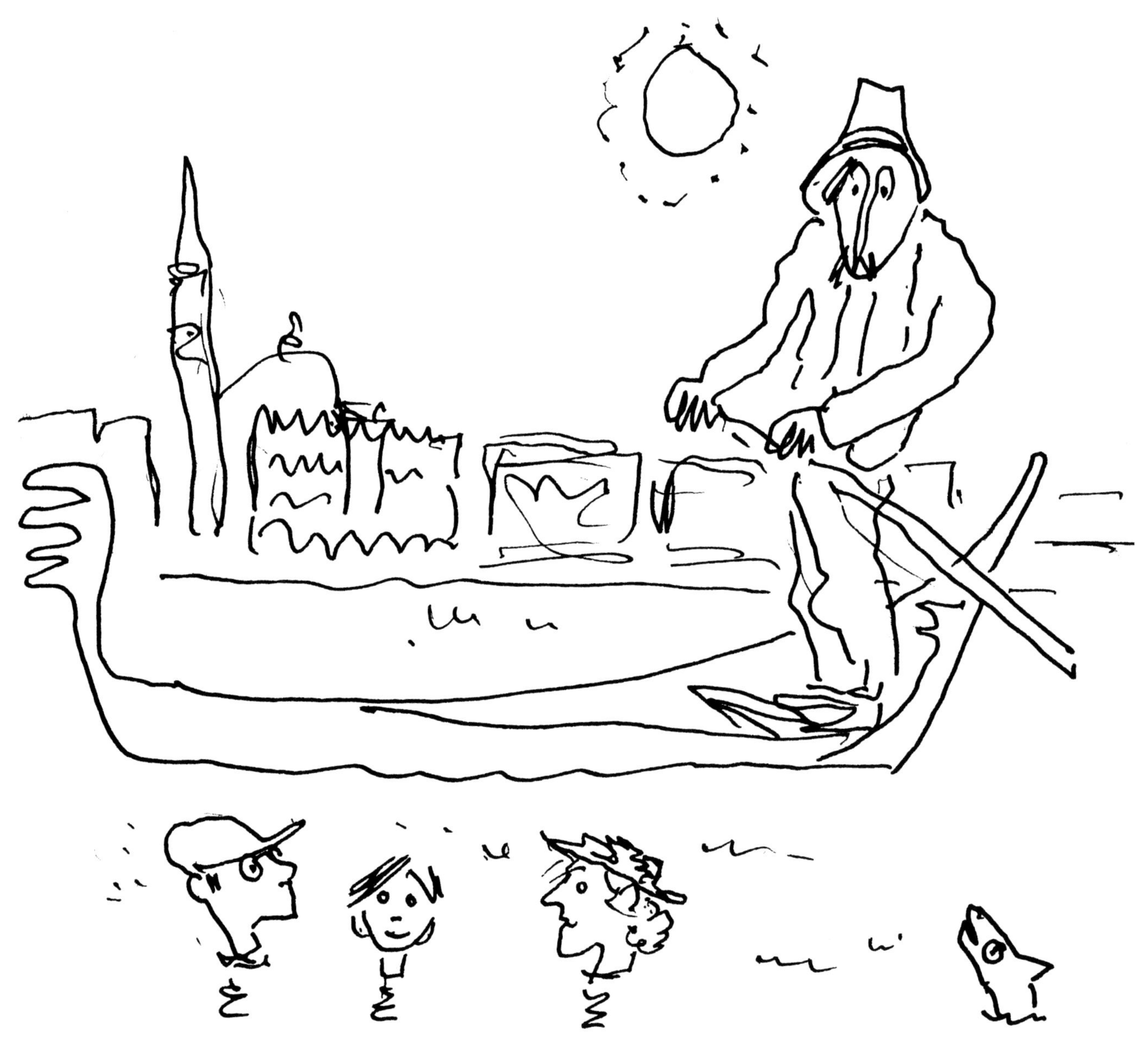

Kyffin, gondola without tourists! (a thank you note to David Meredith)

to him, 'Ivor, I've got a greatcoat in my van, would you like me to pose for you?' He said 'good idea', so I came and stood like Churchill with my hand on a stick in an imposing figure and, actually, I am the figure in Parliament Square. That's me standing there! Of course it has the head of Churchill, but that doesn't matter. It is very fine, very fine. Everybody loves the portrait of Churchill. People who come from Japan and everywhere, they go to have their photographs taken at my feet in fact!

When he died, which must be about five years ago now, I wanted an exhibition, a memorial exhibition of Ivor's work, because he was one of the most important portrait sculptors in the world, and he happened to be a Welshman. We had a wonderful Welsh sculptor in Goscombe John, who was tremendous, but I wanted a major exhibition to show that we in Wales had produced a sculptor of very great merit in Ivor, but no, nothing happened.

DM   Am I correct in saying that Ivor's father was from Aberystwyth?

KW   Yes, he was a solicitor and he also played football for Wales, of which Ivor was very proud. He was a beautiful draughtsman too and the only exhibition of his work after his death took place in a little village in Essex, which is really rather sad. Today, the name of Ivor Roberts Jones means nothing to anybody in Wales.

  And no memorial in Wales to remind us of his talent?

KW   No. But the Welsh Sculptural Trust, they were very good. They commissioned Ivor to do heads of distinguished Welsh people and he has done a tremendous number of those. They're all in the National Museum. People like Lord Cledwyn, Sir Geraint Evans, William Crawshay – masses of them. They're very, very good.

DM   And the sculpture of the Oscar-winning actor Hugh Griffith, from Anglesey?

KW   Yes, here in Ynys Môn, we have Lord Cledwyn and we have Hugh Griffith. They've got one of me, but that's not on show. Lord Cledwyn was a wonderful man and I felt he should be painted but I couldn't paint him because of the rather severe disfiguration of his face, the port-wine birthmark. I always exaggerate everything without knowing it and I didn't want to hurt Cledwyn. I wanted Ivor to do it and I knew Ivor, he was very awkward – he always knew best – so I didn't dare say 'Ivor you really ought to do a head of Cledwyn, he has a magnificent head'; he'd just say 'Oh Kyffin, really'. So anyhow, I was subtle – I'm devious, I'm Welsh you see – I had a word with Cledwyn and asked if I could go there and have a drink with him, in the house. He said, 'Oh yes, certainly, come round.' I asked would he mind if I brought a friend with me? And of course he agreed. I said, 'Well I thought I could

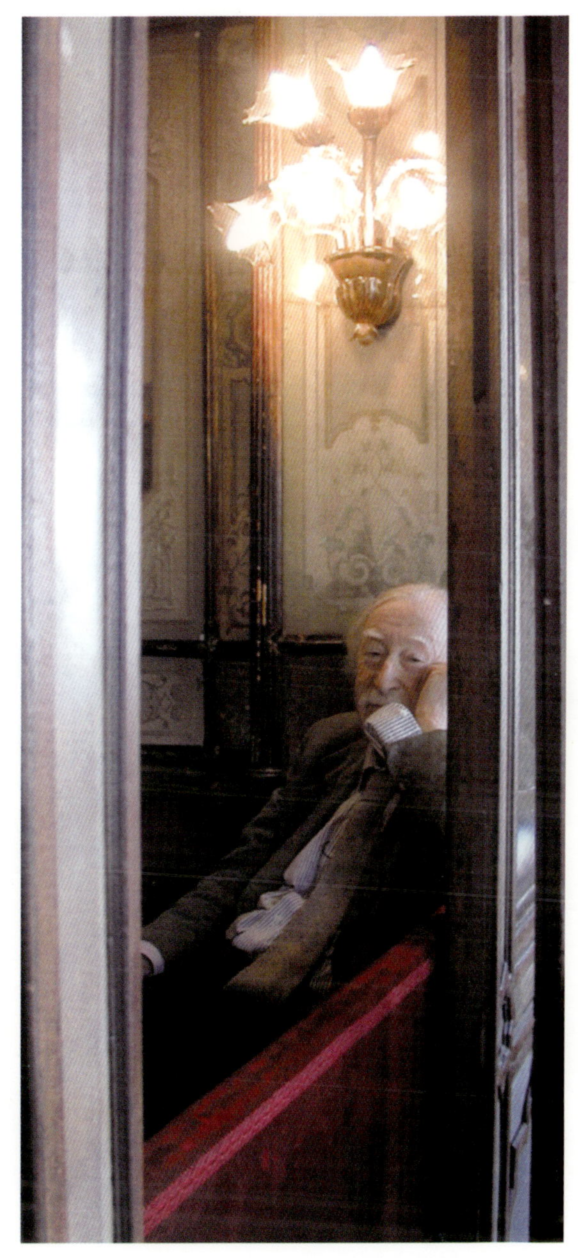

Elegance at Caffè Florian

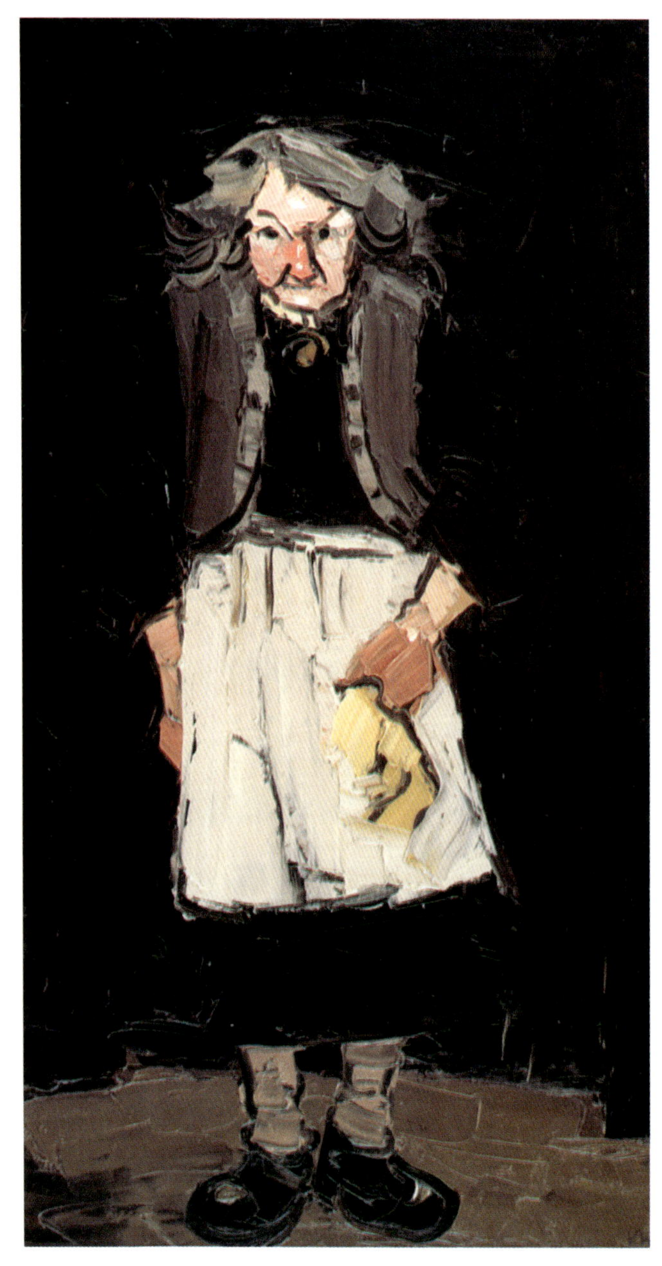

                                           Mrs Hughes

bring Ivor Roberts Jones with me.' And Cledwyn said, 'Fine, I'd like to meet him.' So we went there and within ten minutes Ivor had asked Cledwyn to sit for him. So, that's how that came about.

DM If you were to place one of your paintings on a special pedestal, what would it be?

KW Very, very difficult. I suppose I prefer the best of my portraits – I have one called Mrs Hughes, of an old lady with a duster in her hand. There's another one of Mrs Rowlands of Gerddi Mawr, Llanfair yng Nghornwy. I like those two. But if I had to choose a painting, one painting, it would have to be a picture with a person in it in the landscape, say a farmer and his dog, probably struggling against the elements. I think they're always struggling against the elements. Oh lord, I've painted so much in my life, it's terribly difficult to choose, but I suppose of all the paintings, there are two which I did from Pontllyfni, of a view looking up the Nantlle Valley with snow on the ground and the farmer, quite small, with his dog, and crows in the sky, trying to eat a dead sheep – it's all rather gloomy. But these paintings, I think they'd probably be the ones.

Gratitude

I am very grateful to the following for all
their assistance in so many ways in the
preparation of this book: Mona Roberts for
her thorough transcribing work; Gwenda
Griffith, John Hefin, Stephen Kingston,
Steve Jones, Evan Dobson and Rhodri Glyn
Davies for their photographic contributions;
Sir Idwal Pugh for allowing me to include his
exquisite pencil and watercolour collection
of four Venetian scenes; and Elgan Davies
for designing the book. A special thank
you to everyone involved at Gomer Press,
especially to Bethan Mair, editor of *Kyffin in
Venice*, for her care, inspiration and patience.
My gratitude to Kyffin, in the words of the
prophet, runneth like 'an overflowing stream'.

David Meredith,
Cynllwyd
March 2006

Acknowlegements to photographs

1   'I paint in Welsh'. (Rhodri Glyn Davies)
2   Kyffin Williams and David Meredith at
    Nant Peris, Gwynedd, filming the television
    programme, *Artists*, 1978.
    (personal collection of David Meredith)
3   Kyffin Williams on the Grand Canal.
    (Stephen Kingston)
4   Breakfast at Terrazza Danieli, the restaurant
    overlooking St Mark's Basin and the
    Lagoon, Venice. (John Hefin)
5   Shadows on the canal. (Stephen Kingston)
6   Kyffin Williams prepares for a day's filming
    with Stephen Kingston, cameraman.
    (David Meredith)
7   John Hefin and Gwenda Griffith
    disembarking from vaporetto, Grand Canal.
    (David Meredith)
8   Kyffin Willams sketching at Caffè Florian,
    St Mark's Square, Venice (David Meredith)
9   The camera crew at Caffè Florian.
    (John Hefin)
10 In the water taxi. (Stephen Kingston)
11 Mooring posts, Grand Canal.
    (Stephen Kingston)
12 Paint and palette, Pwllfanogl.
    (Rhodri Glyn Davies)
13 Elegance at the Caffè Florian.
    (Gwenda Griffith)